SKETCH FOR
A HISTORICAL PICTURE OF
THE PROGRESS OF THE
HUMAN MIND

ANTOINE-NICOLAS
DE CONDORCET

SKETCH FOR A HISTORICAL PICTURE OF
THE PROGRESS OF THE
HUMAN MIND

translated by
JUNE BARRACLOUGH

with an Introduction by
STUART HAMPSHIRE
Fellow of New College, Oxford

HYPERION PRESS, INC.
Westport, Connecticut

Published in 1955 by The Noonday Press, New York
Copyright, 1955, by The Noonday Press
Hyperion reprint edition 1979,1988,1991,1992,1993,1994
Library of Congress Catalog Number 78-20458
ISBN 0-88355-838-6
Printed in the United States of America

Library of Congress Cataloging in Publication Data

Condorcet, Marie Jean Antoinne Nicolas Caritat, marquis
de, 1743-1794.
    Sketch for a historical picture of the progress of the
human mind.

    Translation of Esquisse d'un tableau historique des progrès
de l'esprit humain.

    Reprint of the 1955 ed. published by Noonday Press, New
York, in series: Library of Ideas.

    Bibliography: p.
    1. Civilization—Philosophy. 2. Civilization—History.
3. Progress. I. Title. II. Title: The progress of the human mind. III. Series: Library of ideas.
[CB19.C5613 1979b]   190'.9   78-20458
ISBN 0-88355-838-6

CONTENTS

INTRODUCTION

Life and Works

MARIE-JEAN-ANTOINE-NICOLAS CARITAT, Marquis de
Condorcet, was born in 1743 at Ribermont in Picardy. His
father was of noble family, his mother was a bourgeoise.
His father was killed in battle five weeks after he was born,
and he was brought up by his mother, who attended to him
with anxious care and devotion. He was educated by the
Jesuits at the famous Collège de Navarre, where he seems to
have been extremely unhappy. At the age of twenty-two he
submitted to the Académie des sciences his *Essai sur le calcul
integral*, which earned the highest praise from the great
mathematician Lagrange and from d'Alembert. He became a friend of Helvétius and d'Alembert and a member of
the famous society of philosophers and reformers grouped
round Voltaire and the great Encyclopædia. He was a friend
and disciple of Turgot, and learnt from the Physiocrats the
new ideas in political economy, particularly the arguments
for freedom of trade. After the publication of further works
on mathematical analysis and on scientific subjects, he
was elected at the age of twenty-six to the Académie des
sciences; four years later he was elected Secretary of the
Academy, and in 1785 perpetual Secretary. In the next
seventeen years he published an immense variety of treatises
and essays on mathematical, scientific and philosophical subjects. In his capacity as Secretary of the Academy, he wrote
a long series of *éloges* of the famous scientists and writers
of his century, like Fontenelle before him. Taken together,
these *éloges* amount to a survey of the modern knowledge

of his time. In 1782 he was elected to the Académie Française. In his publications during this period he shows that scientific enlightenment and social reform are always linked in his mind; and throughout his life he returned again and again to schemes of popular education. He wrote pamphlets on specific cases of injustice and brutality, on slavery and on the treatment of Protestants in France. As the Revolution came nearer, he was increasingly absorbed in the practical details of politics and in journalism, writing on electoral reform and the abuses of the day, using a variety of pseudonyms, and also speaking at societies and before the many groups of radicals and reformers which were active in France at that time. He married in December 1786 Sophie de Grouchy, a woman of twenty-three, of great charm and brilliance, who made their house in Paris the natural meeting-place of the most distinguished philosophers and radicals of France and of Europe. She survived her husband by many years, maintaining her salon as a personality in her own right, and died in 1822.

In 1789 Condorcet was elected to the Commune of Paris. He was not a member of the Constituent Assembly, but he was active on its margin as a journalist, and particularly in expounding a brilliant and detailed scheme of national education. In 1791 he was elected to the Legislative Assembly, and was one of its most respected figures, finally becoming its president. When his great educational schemes were rejected, he turned his attention to devising a permanent constitution for the Republic; his reports and speeches on this subject are of great length. But the struggle between the Jacobins and the Girondins ended in the destruction of the Girondins, and Condorcet, who had always been opposed to violence and was certainly not a Jacobin, was left with little chance of imposing his constitutional ideas. He wrote and voted against the execution of the king; he declared himself in favour of the most extreme penalty short of death. He was still in June 1793 member of a sub-com-

mittee of the Committee of Public Safety, together with
Robespierre and others. But when a new Jacobin Constitution was adopted by the Convention, he attacked it in a
public letter, as being a constitution imposed by force. He
was forced to hide in the house of a Madame Vernet from
the anger of the Jacobins, who ordered his arrest. While in
hiding he set to work on the *Sketch for a Historical Picture
of the Progress of the Human Mind* which he had long intended to write in a fuller and more detailed form. He
worked from July 1793 to the end of March 1794; he then
decided that he must leave the house and, having failed to
find asylum elsewhere, he was soon identified as an aristo-
crat, arrested for being without papers, and imprisoned at
Bourg-La-Reine. He was found dead in his cell on the
following day; it is possible, but not certain, that he took
poison.

He was a man of gentle and ardent disposition, almost
universally liked and admired, and with a passionate hatred
of injustice. D'Alembert called him 'un volcan couvert de
neige.' There is a vivid portrait of him left by Mlle de
Lespinasse. Visionary and idealistic, he was the type of the
philosopher-reformer of his time.

The Sketch

*L'Esquisse d'un tableau historique des progrès de l'esprit
humain* was in large part written under the threat of death;
it bears the marks of having been written with a great sense
of urgency by a man who wished to draw his thought together, and to leave his testament in a summary form in the
short time still left to him. It stands in need of revision; it is
often repetitive, sometimes obscure and always rhetorical.
But it is one of the few really great monuments of liberal
thought, and it shows far greater insight and originality than
is ordinarily recognized. Its originality has been overlooked
simply because it has been written about and talked about

more often than it has been read. Condorcet was not merely a man who had a noble view of human history and of the possible scope of human improvement through reason and personal liberty; he in fact saw further into the future, and anticipated more of the political, social and international changes of the modern world than did any of his contemporaries.

The idea of history as the story of man's progress from superstition and barbarism to an age of reason and enlightenment was not invented by Condorcet; the same idea is to be found in Voltaire and even more explicitly in Turgot's *Tableau philosophique successif de l'esprit humain*. Condorcet's originality was to extend the doctrine of progress to every department of human activity; he saw history as the story of intellectual, political, economic, social and artistic progress, all necessarily interconnected. Being himself a distinguished mathematician with a genuine knowledge of science, he had a wider view of human culture than anyone who had previously attempted a universal history. 'Up till now, the history of politics . . . has been the history of only a few individuals: that which really constitutes the human race . . . has been forgotten.' It is the duty of the historian to trace the causes which have really affected the mass of human kind. This larger view of history is the strength and originalty of the book, to be set against the naïveté of its view of the Middle Ages and of the inevitable perfection of man in the coming age of reason. Condorcet saw the outlines of liberal democracy more than a century in advance of his time: universal education; universal suffrage; equality before the law; freedom of thought and expression; the right to freedom and self-determination of colonial peoples; the redistribution of wealth; a system of national insurance and pensions; equal rights for women. He deduced this programme of freedom and equality from a doctrine of the. natural rights of man, grounded in man's nature as a being capable of feeling and of reasoning. All men have an equal right to freedom, to the use of their reason and to the pursuit of happiness; when they have been educated, they will inevitably recognize by the light of reason that these natural rights override all other differences between them. They have in the past been prevented from claiming their rights by ignorance and superstition, and tyrants and priests have had an interest in keeping them in ignorance. With the discovery of printing, and the diffusion of scientific knowledge, superstition is being undermined, and will increasingly be undermined in the future. Knowledge and liberty must reinforce each other in an ever-accelerating circle. An enlightened public opinion must ultimately be irresistible. The actual inequality and injustices of the past and present have been due only to ignorance and bad institutions; these bad institutions have been justified by the mistaken philosophy of the social contract or of the division of powers. But, at a high stage of civilized enlightenment, there will come into existence what Condorcet called 'the social art', and politics can be 'a true theory, founded on general principles that are based on nature, and avowed by reason'. If there is no cosmic disaster, we can be certain of continuous progress in enlightenment, freedom and equality. Condorcet accurately foresaw the great power of popular journalism, just beginning in his own day, and of the world-wide diffusion of knowledge and opinion. He foresaw also that statistical methods would be applied in the study of social problems, and that scientific method could be applied to the study of society as the basis of legislation and of social reform.

So much, and more, will be found in these pages, anticipating the radical programme of the next hundred years, and founding the study of politics on the study of history. Condorcet has always been criticized for his too simple and optimistic view of human nature. He adopted without question the advanced philosophical psychology of his time from Condillac; man is governed by pleasure and pain and is capable of reasonable calculation. His 'nature' is good, but he has hitherto been corrupted by tyranny and ignorance. Education in the use of reason will eliminate every vice, if men's sympathies and sensibilities are also properly trained and developed. These simple commonplaces of eighteenth-century thought will be found in the introduction to the *Sketch*; upon them Condorcet founded his now questionable faith in a natural law of human progress. He himself insisted that political programmes, and any system of rights and duties, must be founded upon some analysis of the human heart and of human sentiments. Unlike Rousseau, he made no such analysis for himself, and he had no new insight into the varieties of human needs, and into the less than conscious impulses which may destroy civilizations, and may interrupt the spread of sympathy and reason. This book, conceived only as an introduction to a larger work on the human spirit, was therefore the last monument to a European movement that was coming to an end, at least in the thinness of its assumptions about human nature, its contempt of pre-scientific thought, and its vision of the coming dawn of reason and enlightenment. But it was also the first and most complete statement of that radical programme which was gradually to be translated into fact in the democracies of Western Europe. There are very few works of political thought which have so accurately anticipated the social achievements of the future by more than a century. Condorcet's ideas of history and of natural science had a profound influence on Saint-Simon and Comte, in particular on their dominant notion of the possibility and desirability of the scientific organization of all departments of human life in accordance with a rational scheme. His plans for popular education greatly influenced the French educational system itself.

STUART HAMPSHIRE

A NOTE ON THE TEXT

THE manuscript of the *Sketch* is in the Bibliothèque de l'Institut, Paris (No. 885). This is certainly the work on which Condorcet was engaged when in hiding with Mme Vernet, and, according to the author's note, it was completed 'Friday 4 October 1793 old style, 13th of 1st month of the Year Two of the French Republic'. It was obviously very hastily written, part of it on the backs of proclamations and other sheets of used paper. It is full of mistakes of spelling, punctuation and grammar: corrections are numerous. The manuscript bears the title *Prospectus d'un tableau historique des progrès de l'esprit humain.*

A large number of notes for this work are also to be found in the Bibliothèque de l'Institut as well as in the Bibliothèque nationale. These conclusively show that Condorcet had been planning and preparing it for some time before he went into hiding.

The *Sketch* was first published by the French Republic at its own expense, in an edition of three thousand copies in the Year III (1795). The text varies considerably from the Bibliothèque de l'Institut manuscript and is a great improvement upon it. Whether these alterations, many of which are essential for readability, were made by Condorcet himself in a later draft, by his secretary or by an official of the Republic is not known.

In 1847 Condorcet's complete works were produced. The text of the *Sketch* that appears in Volume VI again differs from that of the Year III. The editor, Arago, says that he has revised the text 'd'après le manuscrit'; but he does not disclose which manuscript. However, as he worked in close collaboration with Mme O'Connor, Condorcet's daughter, he may have used a text in her private possession. The situation is obscure.

The translation presented here follows the Arago text. But in conformity with the practice of Condorcet's modern editor, Professor O. H. Prior, all the passages that are not to be found in the Bibliothèque de l'Institut manuscript have been placed in square brackets.

The only previous English translation appeared anonymously in 1795. It is of poor quality and often inaccurate.

SELECT BIBLIOGRAPHY

A. TEXTS

Esquisse d'un tableau historique des progrès de l'esprit humain.
Ouvrage posthume de Condorcet. Paris, 1795.

Œuvres complètes de Condorcet. Ed. Mme M. L. S. de Condorcet, with the assistance of A. A. Barbier, Cabanis and Garat. 21 vols. Paris, 1804.

Œuvres complètes de Condorcet. Ed. A. Condorcet O'Connor and M. F. Arago. Including a biography of Condorcet by Arago. 12 vols. Paris, 1847.

Condorcet: *Esquisse d'un tableau historique des progrès de l'esprit humain.* Ed. O. H. Prior. Paris, 1933.

Condorcet: *Choix de textes.* Ed. with Introduction by J.-B. Sévérac. (Les grands philosophes Français et étrangers.)

B. WORKS ON CONDORCET

Alengry, Franck: *Condorcet, guide de la Révolution française, théoricien du droit constitutionel et précurseur de la science sociale.* Paris, 1904.

Buisson, F.: *Condorcet.* Paris, 1932.

Cahen, Léon: *Condorcet et la révolution française.* Paris, 1904.

Caillaud, E.: *Les Idées économiques de Condorcet.* Poitiers, 1908.

Comte, Auguste: *Cours de philosophie positive.* Paris, 1892–94, Vol. IV, 47e leçon. *Système de politique positive.* Paris, 1879–83, Vol. IV, Appendice générale.

Delsaux, Hélène: *Condorcet journaliste.* With bibliography. Paris, 1931.

Frazer, Sir James: *Condorcet on the Progress of the Human Mind.* Zaharoff Lecture. Oxford, 1933.

Guillois, Antoine: *La Marquise de Condorcet, sa famille, son salon, ses amis (1764–1822).* Paris, 1867.

Koyré, Alexander: 'Condorcet' in *Journal of the History of Ideas*, Vol. IX, No. 2., April, 1948.

Malthus, T.: *An Essay on the Principles of Population, as it affects the future improvement of Society: with remarks on the speculations of Mr. Godwin, M. Condorcet, and other writers*. London, 1798.

Morley, John: 'Condorcet' in *Critical Miscellanies*, Vol. II. London, 1886.

Robinet, Dr.: *Condorcet, sa vie, son œuvre* (1743-94). Paris, 1895.

Sainte-Beuve, C. A.: 'Condorcet' in *Causeries du Lundi*, Vol. III. Paris, 1852-62.

Schapiro, J. Salwyn: *Condorcet and the Rise of Liberalism*. New York, 1934.

Sée, Henri: 'Condorcet, ses idées et son rôle politique' in *Revue de synthèse historique*, Tome X, 1905.

Vial, Francisque: *Condorcet et l'éducation démocratique*. Paris, 1902.

C. MORE GENERAL WORKS

Becker, C.: *The Heavenly City of the Eighteenth Century Philosophers*. New Haven, 1932.

Bury, J. B.: *Idea of Progress*. London, 1920.

Frankel, Charles: *The Faith of Reason: the Idea of Progress in the French Enlightenment*. New York, 1948.

Martin, Kingsley: *French Liberal Thought in the Eighteenth Century*. Second Edition. London, 1954.

Mornet, Daniel: *Les Origines intellectuelles de la révolution française*. Paris, 1933.

SKETCH FOR
A HISTORICAL PICTURE OF
THE PROGRESS OF THE
HUMAN MIND

INTRODUCTION

MAN is born with the ability to receive sensations; to perceive them and to distinguish between the various simple sensations of which they are composed; to remember, recognize and combine them; to compare these combinations; to apprehend what they have in common and the ways in which they differ; to attach signs to them all in order to recognize them more easily and to allow for the ready production of new combinations.

This faculty is developed in him through the action of external objects, that is to say, by the occurrence of certain composite sensations whose constancy or coherence in change are independent of him; through communication with other beings like himself; and finally through various artificial methods which these first developments have led him to invent.

Sensations are attended by pleasure or pain; and man for his part has the capacity to transform such momentary impressions into permanent feelings of an agreeable or disagreeable character, and then to experience these feelings when he either observes or recollects the pleasures and pains of other sentient beings.

Finally, as a consequence of this capacity and of his ability to form and combine ideas, there arise between him and his fellow-creatures ties of interest and duty, to which nature herself has wished to attach the most precious portion of our happiness and the most painful of our ills.

If one confines oneself to the study and observation of the general facts and laws about the development of these faculties, considering only what is common to all human beings, this science is called metaphysics. But if one studies this development as it manifests itself in the inhabitants of a certain area at a certain period of time and then traces it on from generation to generation, one has the picture of the progress of the human mind. This progress is subject to the same general laws that can be observed in the development of the faculties of the individual, and it is indeed no more than the sum of that development realized in a large number of individuals joined together in society. What happens at any particular moment is the result of what has happened at all previous moments, and itself has an influence on what will happen in the future.

So such a picture is historical, since it is a record of change and is based on the observation of human societies throughout the different stages of their development. It ought to reveal the order of this change and the influence that each moment exerts upon the subsequent moment, and so ought also to show, in the modifications that the human species has undergone, ceaselessly renewing itself through the immensity of the centuries, the path that it has followed, the steps that it has made towards truth or happiness.

Such observations upon what man has been and what he is today, will instruct us about the means we should employ to make certain and rapid the further progress that his nature allows him still to hope for.

Such is the aim of the work that I have undertaken, and its result will be to show by appeal to reason and fact that nature has set no term to the perfection of human faculties; that the perfectibility of man is truly indefinite; and that the progress of this perfectibility, from now onwards independent of any power that might wish to halt it, has no other limit than the duration of the globe upon which nature has cast us. This progress will doubtless vary in speed, but it will never be reversed as long as the earth occupies its present place in the system of the universe, and as long as the general laws of this system produce neither a general cataclysm nor such changes as will deprive the human race of its present faculties and its present resources.

The first stage of civilization observed amongst human beings is that of a small society whose members live by hunting and fishing, and know only how to make rather crude weapons and household utensils and to build or dig for themselves a place in which to live, but are already in possession of a language with which to communicate their needs, and a small number of moral ideas which serve as common laws of conduct; living in families, conforming to general customs which take the place of laws, and even possessing a crude system of government.

The uncertainty of life, the difficulty man experiences in providing for his needs, and the necessary cycle of extreme activity and total idleness do not allow him the leisure in which he can indulge in thought and enrich his understanding with flew combinations of ideas. The means of satisfying his needs are too dependent on chance and the seasons to encourage any occupation whose progress might be handed down to later generations, and so each man confines himself to perfecting his own individual skill and talent.

Thus the progress of the human species was necessarily very slow; it could move forward only from time to time when it was favoured by exceptional circumstances. However, we see hunting, fishing and the natural fruits of the earth replaced as a source of subsistence by food obtained from animals that man domesticates and that he learns to keep and to breed. Later, a primitive form of agriculture developed; man was no longer satisfied with the fruits or plants that he came across by chance, but learnt to store them, to collect them around his dwelling, to sow or plant them, and to provide them with favourable conditions under which they could spread.

Property, which at first was limited to the animals that a man killed, his weapons, his nets and his cooking utensils,

later came to include his cattle and eventually was extended
to the earth that he won from its virgin state and cultivated.
On the death of the owner this property naturally passed
into the hands of his family, and in consequence some people
came to possess a surplus that they could keep. If this
surplus was absolute, it gave rise to new needs; but if it existed only in one commodity and at the same time there was
a scarcity of another, this state of affairs naturally suggested
the idea of exchange, and from then onwards, moral relations grew in number and increased in complexity. A life
that was less hazardous and more leisured gave opportunities for meditation or, at least, for sustained observation.
Some people adopted the practice of exchanging part of
their surplus for labour from which they would then be ab-
solved. In consequence there arose a class of men whose
time was not wholly taken up in manual labour and whose
desires extended beyond their elementary needs. Industry
was born; the arts that were already known, were spread and
perfected; as men became more experienced and attentive,
quite casual information suggested to them new arts; the
population grew as the means of subsistence became less
dangerous and precarious; agriculture, which could support
a greater number of people on the same amount of land,
replaced the other means of subsistence; it encouraged the
growth of the population and this, in its turn, favoured
progress; acquired ideas were communicated more quickly
and were perpetuated more surely in a society that had
become more sedentary, more accessible and more intimate.
Already, the dawn of science had begun to break; man
revealed himself to be distinct from the other species of
animals and seemed no longer confined like them to a
purely individual perfection.

As human relations increased in number, scope and complexity, it became necessary to have a method of communicating with those who were absent, of perpetuating
the memory of an event with greater precision than that

afforded by oral tradition, of fixing the terms of an agreement with greater certainty than that assured by the testimony of witnesses, and of registering in a more enduring manner those respected customs according to which the members of a single society had agreed to regulate their conduct. So the need for writing was felt, and writing was invented. It seems to have been at first a genuine system of representation, but this gave way to a more conventional representation which preserved merely the characteristic features of objects. Finally by a sort of metaphor analogous to that which had already been introduced into language, the image of a physical object came to express moral ideas. The origin of these signs, like that of words, was ultimately forgotten, and writing became the art of attaching a conventional sign to every idea, to every word, and so by extension, to every modification of ideas and words.

And so mankind had both a written and spoken language, both of which had to be learnt and between which an equivalence had to be established.

Certain men of genius, humanity's eternal benefactors, whose names and country are for ever buried in oblivion, observed that all the words of a language were nothing but the combinations of a very limited number of primary sounds, but that their number, though very limited, was enough to form an almost limitless number of different combinations. They devised the notion of using visible signs to designate not the ideas or the words that corresponded to ideas, but the simple elements of which words are composed. And here we have the origin of the alphabet; a small number of signs sufficed to write everything, just as a small number of sounds sufficed to say everything. The written language was the same as the spoken language; all that was necessary was to know how to recognize and reproduce these few signs, and this final step assured the progress of the human race for ever.

[Perhaps it would be useful today to invent a written

language that, reserved exclusively for the sciences, expressing only the combinations of those simple ideas which are the same for every mind, and used only for the reasoning of strict logic, for the precise and calculated operations of the understanding, would be understood by the people of every country and could be translated into every vernacular and would not have to be altered, as happens now, when it passed into general use.]

[So by a strange revolution this type of writing, whose survival would only have helped to prolong ignorance, would now become, in the hands of philosophy, a useful tool for the swift propagation of enlightenment and for the perfection of scientific method.]

All peoples whose history is recorded fall somewhere between our present degree of civilization and that which we still see amongst savage tribes; if we survey in a single sweep the universal history of peoples we see them sometimes making fresh progress, sometimes plunging back into ignorance, sometimes surviving somewhere between these extremes or halted at a certain point, sometimes disappearing from the earth under the conqueror's heel, mixing with the victors or living on in slavery, or sometimes receiving knowledge from some more enlightened people in order to transmit it in their turn to other nations, and so welding an uninterrupted chain between the beginning of historical time and the century in which we live, between the first peoples known to us and the present nations of Europe.

So the picture that I have undertaken to sketch falls into three distinct parts.

In the first our information is based on the tales that travellers bring back to us about the state of the human race among the less civilized peoples, and we have to conjecture the stages by which man living in isolation or restricted to the kind of association necessary for survival, was able to make the first steps on a path whose destination is the use of a developed language. This is the most important distinction and indeed, apart from a few more extensive ideas of morality and the feeble beginnings of social order, the only one separating man from the animals who like him live in a regular and continuous society. We are therefore in this matter forced to rely upon theoretical observations about the development of our intellectual and moral faculties.

In order to carry the history of man up to the point where he practises certain arts, where knowledge of the sciences has already begun to enlighten him, where trade unites the nations and where, finally, alphabetical writing is invented, we can add to this first guide the history of the different societies which have been observed in all their intermediary stages, although none can be traced back far enough to enable us to bridge the gulf which separates these two great eras of the human race.

Here the picture begins to depend in large part on a succession of facts transmitted to us in history, but it is necessary to select them from the history of different peoples, to compare them and combine them in order to extract the hypothetical history of a single people and to compose the picture of its progress.

The history of man from the time when alphabetical writing was known in Greece to the condition of the human race at the present day in the most enlightened countries of Europe is linked by an uninterrupted chain of facts and observations; and so at this point the picture of the march and progress of the human mind becomes truly historical. Philosophy has nothing more to guess, no more hypothetical surmises to make; it is enough to assemble and order the facts and to show the useful truths that can be derived from their connections and from their totality.

When we have shown all this, there will remain one last picture for us to sketch: that of our hopes, and of the progress reserved for future generations, which the constancy of the laws of nature seems to assure them. It will be necessary to indicate by what stages what must appear to us today a fantastic hope ought in time to become possible, and even likely; to show why, in spite of the transitory successes of prejudice and the support that it receives from the corruption of governments or peoples, truth alone will obtain a lasting victory; we shall demonstrate how nature has joined together indissolubly the progress of knowledge and that of liberty, virtue and respect for the natural rights of man; and how these, the only real goods that we possess, though so often separated that they have even been held to be incompatible, must on the contrary become inseparable from the moment when enlightenment has attained a certain level in a number of nations, and has penetrated throughout the whole mass of a great people whose language is universally known and whose commercial relations embrace the whole area of the globe. Once such a close accord had been established between all enlightened men, from then onwards all will be the friends of humanity, all will work together for its perfection and its happiness.

We shall reveal the origin and trace the history of those widespread errors which have somewhat retarded or suspended the progress of reason and which have, as often as forces of a political character, even caused man to fall back into ignorance.

The operations of the understanding that lead us into error or hold us there, from the subtle paralogism which can deceive even the most enlightened of men, to the dreams of a madman, belong no less than the methods of right reasoning or of discourse to the theory of the development of our individual faculties; on the same principle, the way in which general errors are insinuated amongst peoples and are propagated, transmitted and perpetuated is all part of the historical picture of the progress of the human mind. Like the truths that perfect and illuminate it, they are the necessary consequences of its activity and of the disproportion that for ever holds between what it knows, what it wishes to know and what it believes it needs to know.

It can even be observed that, according to the general laws of the development of our faculties, certain prejudices have necessarily come into being at each stage of our progress, but they have extended their seductions or their empire long beyond their due season, because men retain the prejudices of their childhood, their country and their age, long after they have discovered all the truths necessary to destroy them.

Finally, in all countries at all times there are different prejudices varying with the standard of education of the different classes of men and their professions. The prejudices of philosophers harm the progress of truth; those of the less enlightened classes retard the propagation of truths already known; those of certain eminent or powerful professions place obstacles in truth's way: here we see three enemies whom reason is obliged to combat without respite, and whom she vanquishes often only after a long and painful struggle. The history of these struggles, of the birth, triumph and fall of prejudices will occupy a great part of this work and will be neither the least important nor the least useful section of it.

[If there is to be a science for predicting the progress of the human race, for directing and hastening it, the history of the progress already achieved must be its foundation.]

[Philosophy has had to proscribe in no uncertain terms that superstition which believes that rules of conduct can be found only in the history of past centuries, and truth only in the study of ancient opinions. But ought it not to condemn with equal vigour the prejudice that arrogantly rejects the lessons of experience? Without doubt it is only by meditation, which furnishes us with fruitful combinations of ideas, that we can arrive at any general truths in the science of man. But if the study of individual human beings is useful to the metaphysician and the moralist, why should the study of societies be any less useful to them and to the political philosopher; If it is useful to observe the various societies that exist side by side, and to study the relations between them, why should it not also be useful to observe them across the passage of time? Even if we suppose that these observations can be neglected in the search for speculative truths, ought they to be ignored when it is a question of applying these truths in practice and of deducing from science the art which should be its useful result? Do not our prejudices and the evils that proceed from them have their origins in the prejudices of our ancestors? Is not one of the most certain ways of undeceiving ourselves from the one and of guarding ourselves against the other, to study their origins and their effects?]

[Are we now at the stage when we have nothing further to fear, neither new errors nor the return of old ones; when no corrupting institution can any longer be devised by hypocrisy, and adopted by ignorance or enthusiasm; when no evil combination can any longer ruin a great nation? Would it then be useless to know how in the past nations have been deceived, corrupted or plunged into misery?]

[Everything tells us that we are now close upon one of the great revolutions of the human race. If we wish to learn what to expect from it and to procure a certain guide to lead us in the midst of its vicissitudes, what could be more suitable than to have some picture of the revolutions that have gone before it and prepared its way? The present state of enlightenment assures us that this revolution will have a favourable result, but is not this only on condition that we know how to employ our knowledge and resources to their fullest extent? And in order that the happiness that it promises may be less dearly bought, that it may be diffused more rapidly over a greater area, that it may be more complete in its effects, do we not need to study the history of the human spirit to discover what obstacles we still have to fear and what means are open to us of surmounting them?]

I shall divide the area that I propose to cover into nine great stages [and in a tenth I shall venture to offer some observations on the future destiny of the human race].

[I shall confine myself here to presenting the main features that characterize each of these stages; I shall deal only with the outlines, and not stop to mention exceptions or details.]

[I shall point out the subjects and the conclusions; the work itself will offer the development and the proof.]

THE FIRST STAGE

Men are united in tribes

TRIBAL society is the first stage in human history about which we have any direct observation; and therefore, if we wish to conjecture how man arrived at this degree of civilization, we can do so only by examining his intellectual and moral qualities and his physical constitution.

A few observations about the physical qualities of man that might have favoured the original formation of society, and a brief analysis of the development of our intellectual and moral faculties would, then, be appropriate as an introduction to the picture of this stage.

A family society seems to be natural to man. Its origin is to be found in the child's need for its parents and in the natural solicitude of the mother and—though to a lesser extent—of the father for their offspring. But the child's need lasts long enough to bring into existence and foster a desire to perpetuate this life together and to awaken a lively sense of its advantages. A family that lived in a region offering ready means of subsistence could increase and become a tribe.

Those tribes which arose as a result of the association of several separate families represent a later and less common phenomenon, since associations of this sort are prompted by motives of less urgency and depend upon the concurrence of a greater number of circumstances.

The first fruits of continuous association are a number of arts, all concerned with the satisfaction of simple needs. They include the making of weapons, cooking and the construction of the utensils necessary for cooking, preserving food and providing against those times of the year when fresh supplies are unobtainable: it is these arts that first serve to distinguish human society from that formed by various species of animals.

In some of these tribes the women grew edible plants around their huts and these supplemented the produce of hunting and fishing. In others which lived where the earth in its natural state supplied vegetation that can be eaten, the finding and gathering of this food occupied part of the time of these primitive peoples. In these latter cases where the advantages of association were less obvious, we find civilization reduced almost to the simple family society. However, the use of developed language seems universal.

More frequent and stable intercourse between people, the identity of their interests, and the help that they gave one another in communal hunting and defence against an enemy must have produced in equal measure the sentiment of justice and mutual affection between the members of the same society. Soon this affection developed into an attachment to the society itself: and this, in its turn, gave rise to violent hatred of the enemies of the tribe and an inextinguishable thirst for revenge.

The tribe needed to act in concert for the purpose of self-defence or to facilitate the task of acquiring more assured and more abundant means of subsistence. And this situation, which created the necessity for a leader, introduced the first ideas of political authority into these societies. In all matters of common interest which called for a common decision, all those who were expected to execute the decision had to be consulted. Women who were prevented from taking part in long expeditions and war because of their weakness were by the same token excluded from the general councils, which usually had to do with such matters. As their decisions required experience, only those were admitted to consultations who might be assumed to have it. Any disagreement arising within the bosom of a single society would disturb its harmony and might even bring about its destruction; and so it was natural that decisions should become the responsibility of those who by reason of their age or personal qualities inspired the greatest confidence.

Such were the beginnings of political institutions.

The formation of language must have preceded these institutions. The idea of expressing objects by conventional signs may seem above the reach of human intelligence at this stage of civilization, but it is likely that such signs were introduced into common use as the work of time, by degrees, almost imperceptibly.

The invention of the bow was the work of a single man of genius, the formation of language was that of the whole society. These two kinds of progress are equally characteristic of human genius. The one, more swift in its operation, is the result of new combinations of ideas that men favoured by nature are able to form, it is the prize of their meditations and their efforts; the other, a slower process, is born of the reflections and observations that offer themselves to all men and even from the habits that they contract in the course of their life together.

[Measured and regular movements can be performed with less fatigue; and their order and arrangement can be understood more easily by those who watch or listen to them. They are for these two reasons a source of pleasure. And thus it is that we can trace the origin of the dance, of music, and of poetry to the early infancy of society. The dance is employed for the entertainment of the young and on occasions of public rejoicing. We also find love songs and songs of battle, and people even know how to make a few musical instruments. The art of eloquence is not absolutely unknown in these tribes; at any rate in ceremonial speeches a graver and more solemn note is struck; and even rhetorical exaggeration is no stranger to them.]

Vengeance and cruelty towards enemies erected into virtues; the opinion that condemns women to a sort of slavery; the right to command in battle regarded as the prerogative of one family; and the first notions of the various kinds of superstition—such are the errors that distinguish this stage, and it must be our task to trace their origins and to discover their motives. For man does not adopt without reason an error which has not been made to seem quite natural by his early upbringing; if he does adopt any new errors, it must be because they are linked with the errors of his childhood and because his interests, passions or opinions, or the course of events have disposed him to receive them.

Some crude knowledge of astronomy and of certain medicinal plants used in sickness or for curing wounds are the only sciences known to these savages, and these are already corrupted by an admixture of superstition.

But, nevertheless, this stage confronts us with a fact that is important in the history of the human mind. We can detect the first signs of an institution which has had contrary effects upon human progress; which has accelerated the progress of reason at the same time as it has propagated error; which has enriched science with new truths whilst it has plunged the people into ignorance and religious servitude, and which has brought transitory benefits at the price of a long and degrading tyranny.

I refer to the formation of a class of men who are the depositaries of the principles of the sciences or the procedures of the arts, of the mysteries or ceremonies of religion, of the practices of superstition, and often even of the secrets of legislation and politics. I refer to the separation of the human race into two parts; the one destined to teach, the other made to believe; the one jealously hiding what it boasts of knowing, the other receiving with respect whatever is condescendingly revealed to it; the one wishing to place itself above reason, the other humbly renouncing its own

c

reason and abasing itself to less than human stature by acknowledging in others prerogatives that would place them above their common nature.

This distinction whose relics we are still now offered by priests at the end of the eighteenth century, is found amongst the least civilized savages who already have their charlatans and their sorcerers. It is a distinction so general, one meets with it so constantly in all stages of civilization that it must have a foundation in nature itself; and thus we shall discover in our examination of the faculties of man in the early days of society the cause of the credulity of the original dupes, and the cause of the crude cunning of the original impostors.

THE SECOND STAGE

Pastoral peoples:
The transition from this stage to that
of agricultural peoples

THE idea of keeping in captivity the animals caught in hunting must have occurred very naturally to man: what was required was that they should be tame enough to be kept without difficulty, that there should be ample facilities for grazing, that the family should have more food than it could eat itself or, alternatively, that it should live in fear of famine through failure in hunting or through the inclemency of the seasons.

At first the animals were kept merely as a reserve or larder, but it was soon found that they could breed and so provide a more lasting means of subsistence. Their milk was an addition to the diet of early man; so that, though at first regarded only as a supplement to the produce of the hunt, they soon proved to be a source of supply that was more certain, more abundant and more easily come by. Accordingly hunting ceased to be the principal means of subsistence, and, in the end, to be one at all: it survived only as a pastime and as a much needed way of protecting the herds against wild beasts, for the herds had now become so large that they could not find enough to eat near the tribal dwellings.

A more sedentary and less strenuous form of life afforded man leisure, and this in turn favoured the development of the human mind. When men were certain of their sustenance, and were no longer anxious about their elementary needs, they looked for new sensations in the means of satisfying them.

The arts made some progress; some knowledge was acquired about the feeding of domestic animals, the encouragement of their reproduction, and even about the improvement of strains.

Men discovered the use of wool, and now wore clothes instead of skins.

Family society became gentler without becoming any less intimate. As the herds of the various families bred at different rates, differences in wealth appeared. Then the idea arose whereby one man shared his flocks and herds with another who had none, and this other devoted his time and energy to looking after them. It was noticed that the labour of a young person in good health was worth more than was strictly necessary for his keep, and it became the custom to take prisoners of war as slaves instead of butchering them.

Hospitality in this pastoral stage of history was practised more formally than it had been in earlier times, and was an important solemnity even among peoples who roamed about in waggons or moved with their tents. There were more opportunities for practising hospitality between individuals, between families and between tribes. This act of common humanity became a social duty and was made subject to rules.

Then, as some families had an assured subsistence and even a constant surplus and other men lacked the bare necessities of life, natural compassion for the less fortunate gave rise to the sentiment and habit of benevolence. Manners became less harsh, the slavery of women lost some of its rigour and the wives of the rich were exempted from arduous work.

Greater variety in the articles used to satisfy different wants and in the instruments used to make them, and greater inequality in distribution enlarged the scope of barter and gave rise to genuine trade. This process could not develop without revealing the necessity for a common measure and for some form of money.

Tribes became more numerous; at the same time their dwellings, when they were fixed, tended to be situated farther apart from one another so that the herds could feed more easily; though once they had discovered that some of the animals that they had tamed could be used for carrying or dragging heavy loads, they kept their camps on the move and settled anywhere only briefly.

Each nation had a warrior chieftain, and as the nation was made up of different tribes, each tribe had its chieftain. In almost all cases this honour belonged to certain families. The heads of families who owned large herds and many slaves, and employed many poorer men, shared the authority of the leaders of the tribe, just as the latter shared their authority with the leaders of the nation when age, experience and military repute merited that honour. It is to this stage of society's development that we can trace the origin of slavery and of the inequality of political rights between grown men.

Disputes, which became steadily more numerous and more complicated, were settled by the decisions of the heads of families or the tribal chieftains either by the light of natural reason or in accordance with traditional usage. The body of these judgments, which bore witness to customary usage and saw that it was perpetuated, soon constituted what was in effect a system of traditional law sufficiently consistent and well defined to meet the growing needs of society. The notion of property and of the rights of property was defined more precisely, and its field enlarged. The rights of inheritance became more important and so had to be governed by a fixed code. Agreements were contracted more frequently and they concerned a larger number of issues; they had therefore to be subject to formal rules. The manner in which these agreements were promulgated had also its rules so as to ensure their proper execution.

There was some slight progress in astronomy which can be ascribed to the practical value of this study and to the occupation it afforded shepherds during the long, eventless watches of the night.

At the same time, however, we see the art of deceiving men in order to rob them, of dominating their minds by playing upon their hopes and fears brought to perfection. Some regularity was introduced into the offices of religion; systems of belief were purged of their grosser elements; and men refined to some extent their ideas about the supernatural. We see as a concomitant the advent of pontiff princes, and, in some places, families or tribes devoted to sacerdotal duties, and elsewhere colleges of priests. These differences of form concealed the same phenomenon: a class of individuals who affected insolent prerogatives, who separated themselves from the common mass of mankind so that they might dominate them more effectively, and who sought to gain an exclusive control over medicine and astronomy so that they might hold in their own hands all the means of subjugating the human mind and deprive mankind of any way of unmasking their hypocrisy or destroying their tyranny.

[Languages became richer without becoming less figurative or less bold. The metaphors employed were more varied and more agreeable; they were taken from pastoral and forest life, from the regular cycle of the seasons and from nature's more violent manifestations. One consequence of increased leisure was an audience that was more tranquil and attentive and for that reason more difficult to please, and so song, musical instruments and poetry were perfected. Another consequence was that men could now for the first time observe their own feelings, judge their thoughts critically and select some in preference to others.]

Men must have discovered by observation that some

plants provided better or more abundant food for the herds than others. The utility of concentrating on the cultivation of these and of separating them from plants that were poor, unhealthy or even dangerous to eat was recognized, and ways of achieving this were discovered. Similarly, in countries where plants, cereals and the natural fruits of the earth could contribute to human diet, people presumably studied these plants, observed how they grew, and began to plant them near their dwellings, to separate them from weeds and to protect them from wild beasts and the greed of strangers. Such ideas must have arisen earlier in the more fertile parts of the earth where nature of herself produced almost enough for human needs. In this way men began to devote themselves to agriculture.

It is clear that in a fertile country with a favourable climate, a piece of land can support far more people if it produces cereal, fruit and roots than it would do if it were used as pasture. So when the soil was not too difficult to cultivate, when the beasts of burden had been trained to work on the land, and when agricultural tools had been somewhat improved, farming was able to offer an abundant subsistence and it became the principal occupation of men; and with this the human race reached its third stage.

Some peoples have remained since time immemorial in one or other of the two stages that we have just examined. They have made no progress by their own efforts, but nor have they been affected fundamentally by intercourse or trade with peoples of a very high degree of civilization. They have acquired by these means a little knowledge, some skill and above all many vices, but they have not been roused from their condition of apathy. The principal causes of this backwardness have been climate and custom; the pleasures of an almost perfect independence, which will reappear only in a society more advanced than anything we have yet attained; the natural attachment that men feel towards opinions instilled in childhood and the customs of their country; the natural aversion of ignorance to anything that is new and strange; the indolence of body and mind which crushes the first weak stirrings of curiosity; and, finally, the power wielded by superstition even in the infancy of society. But we must also take into account the greed, cruelty, corruption and prejudice of civilized nations. For these may well seem to primitive races to be richer, more powerful, more educated and more active than they, but also more depraved, and, above all, unhappier; and so savages, instead of being impressed by the superiority of civilized nations, must often have been terrified by the extent and multiplicity of their needs, by the torments they suffer through avarice, and by the eternal agitation of their always active and never satisfied desires. Some philosophers have pitied these savages, whilst others have praised them; what to some seem like wisdom and virtue, are by others branded as stupidity and idleness.

The issue between these opposed attitudes will be resolved in the course of this book. We shall see why the progress of the mind has not always resulted in the progress of society towards happiness and virtue; how the combination of prejudice and error has polluted the good that should flow from knowledge but that depends more on its purity than on its extent. We shall see that the rough and stormy passage from a crude state of society to that degree of civilization enjoyed by enlightened and free nations is in no way a degeneration of the human race but is rather a necessary crisis in its gradual progress towards absolute perfection. And finally we shall see that it is not the growth of knowledge but its decadence that has engendered the vices of civilized peoples, and that knowledge, so far from corrupting man, has always improved him when it could not totally correct or reform him.

The progress of agricultural peoples up to the invention of the alphabet

THE picture that we have been sketching is from now onwards to lose its uniformity. We no longer have a number of tribes distinguished only by slight differences in manners, characteristics, opinions and superstitions, but all alike in being attached to the soil and in preserving the pure strain of some primordial family.

Invasions, conquests and the rise and fall of empires are soon to scatter tribes over new territory or to people a single area with different tribes.

The operation of chance will upset the slow but regular march of nature, often retarding it, sometimes accelerating it.

A phenomenon occuring in one country in such-and-such a century is often the effect of some revolution that took place a thousand leagues away, a thousand years before. Many of these events have been engulfed in the night of time, but their influence can be seen in the lives of our forefathers and sometimes even in our own.

But we must first consider the effects of this change upon a single nation, independently of the influence of wars, invasions and the mixture of peoples.

Agriculture binds men to the earth they cultivate. It was no longer possible for them to wander freely with their families and their hunting implements, driving their cattle before them; nor was there any longer unoccupied territory to provide food for them and for the animals on which they depended during their migrations.

Each piece of land had its master, and it was to him that its fruits belonged. When the harvest brought in more than had been spent to obtain it, more even than was necessary to feed and maintain the men and animals who had toiled to produce it, the owner of the land was provided with a source of wealth that he had obtained without labour.

In the first two stages of society, any man, or at least any family, was able to exercise almost all the essential arts. But once men were divided into those who lived off the produce of their land without working and others who lived by selling their labour for wages, and once new crafts and more complicated techniques had been developed, some kind of division of labour was seen to be necessary in the interests of all. It was found that a man's work improved more rapidly if it was limited in scope; that a small number of movements could be carried out with great speed and accuracy once habit had made them familiar; and that it needed less intelligence to do something well if it had been done time and time again.

So while one section of the community devoted itself to agriculture, another made agricultural tools. The supervision of animals, the management of the household and the manufacture of clothes became separate occupations. Where the family possessed only a very small amount of land, one of these tasks was not by itself enough to occupy one person's time, and so several people shared the work and the wages of one. Soon, the arts were extended to new materials which demanded different procedures, and those that were similar formed separate types of work and to each a particular class of workers attached itself. Trade increased, embracing more commodities and bringing them from farther afield, and so a new class of men was formed, occupied solely in buying commodities, storing them, transporting them and then selling them at a profit.

So to the three existing classes that we can already distinguish in pastoral society, owners, servants attached to the family, and slaves, we must now add workers of every kind, and merchants.

As society became more fixed, more close-knit, more complex, the need was felt for a more regular and more extensive form of law. Greater precision was required in settling the punishment of crime, the forms of customary agreements, and stricter rules were needed for determining the facts to which the laws were to be applied. [This progress was the slow and gradual product of need and circumstance, and it takes us a few steps farther along the road that we have already followed with the pastoral peoples.]

[In the first stages of society, education was purely domestic. Children were educated by their fathers, either by working with them, or by being instructed by them in such arts as they knew; they received from them the small stock of traditions that made up the history of the tribe or of the family; they learnt the various myths that were preserved; and they acquired a knowledge of the national customs, principles or prejudices which constituted a crude moral code. Songs and dances and military exercises were learnt in the company of friends.]

[At this stage of society, the children of the richer families received a kind of communal education either in the towns through the conversation of their elders or in the household of some chief to whom they were attached. There they were instructed in the laws of the country, its customs and its prejudices and they learnt to sing the verses in which their history had been recorded.]

[A more sedentary form of life established a greater equality between the sexes. Women were no longer considered merely as useful objects, slaves in all but their proximity to their master. Men came to see them more as companions, and finally learnt how much they could contribute towards masculine happiness. However, even in the countries where they were most respected and where polygamy was forbidden, reason and justice were not pursued to the extent of a complete reciprocity of duties, nor was equality admitted either in the right of separation or in the punishments for infidelity.]

[The history of this form of prejudice and its influence on the fate of the human race must figure in the picture that I have undertaken; and nothing will serve better to show the extent to which happiness depends upon the progress of reason.]

Some nations remained scattered over the countryside; others were united in towns where there lived the nation's chieftain, the tribal chieftains who shared his power, and the elders of each family. There people stored their most valuable possessions in order to escape the clutches of the robbers who inevitably became more numerous as wealth accumulated. So long as nations remained dispersed, custom fixed a place and a time for the chieftains' meetings, for deliberations on matters of common interest and for the tribunals that pronounced judgment.

Nations that recognized a common origin and spoke a common language nearly always formed a more or less intimate federation without renouncing their warlike habits. They made agreements to unite either in defence against foreign enemies or for the revenge of common wrongs or in the joint performance of some religious duty.

Hospitality and trade brought about a regular intercourse even between tribes of different origins, customs and language; and this intercourse, though interrupted frequently by robbery and war, was on each occasion renewed out of necessity, a force stronger than the love of plunder and the thirst for vengeance. The massacre of the conquered, the confiscation of their possessions and their enslavement were no longer the only rights recognized between warring nations: the surrender of land, ransoms and tribute partly took the place of such barbaric atrocities.

At this stage, anyone who possessed arms was a soldier; whoever had the best weapons and the most experience in handling them and could also supply others with arms and could provision them out of his own stocks inevitably became a chieftain; but the almost voluntary obedience accorded to him contained nothing of servile dependence.

Since there was seldom any necessity for new laws; since there was no public expenditure towards which citizens were obliged to contribute, or if there ever was any expenditure, it was the property of the chief or the common land that bore the burden of it; since the idea of restricting industry and commerce had not yet come into existence; since aggressive wars were undertaken by general consent, or fought solely by volunteers inspired by the love of glory and the desire for plunder, men felt themselves to be free living under these rudimentary governments, despite the hereditary nature of the greater chieftainships, which was almost universal, and the prerogative, unjustly claimed by the lesser chiefs, of sharing in political authority to the exclusion of others and of exercising the functions of administration and the magistrature.

Often, however, a chieftain would indulge in acts of personal vengeance and arbitrary violence; and within the privileged families, pride and faction, unbridled passion and the thirst for gold swelled the number of such crimes. The chieftains who lived in the towns became the instruments of the passions of their royal masters; they stirred up dissension and civil war, they oppressed the people by their injustices, and they plagued them with their villainies and ambitions.

In many nations the excesses of these ruling families exhausted the patience of the masses. They were deposed and hounded out of the country, or else made to submit to common law; though it was rare for them to be allowed to keep their title with an authority thus limited by common law, and the result was usually the establishment of what we now call republics. In other cases these kings, supported by powerful satellites, and with arms and money to distribute to their followers, exercised an absolute authority: such was the origin of tyranny.

In other countries, particularly in those where there were small tribes not living in towns, the primitive and rudimentary constitutions were retained until the people either fell beneath the yoke of some conqueror, or, themselves fired by the spirit of conquest, swarmed out over neighbouring lands.

Tyranny of this kind was necessarily limited to a small area and therefore in all cases was short-lived. The people soon shook off the yoke which force alone had imposed and which even public approval would have been powerless to maintain. The monster, tyranny, was seen at too close quarters not to inspire more loathing than fear; and force cannot, like opinion, endure for long unless the tyrant extends his empire far enough afield to hide from the people, whom he divides and rules, the secret that real power lies not with the oppressors but with the oppressed.

The history of republics belongs to the next stage, but our present study now leads us to a new phenomenon.

In the agricultural stage, a community does not take flight when defeated in war, but is obliged under duress to stay where it is and work for the conqueror. When this happens, the conquering nation is often content to assign captains and soldiers to govern the conquered territories, protect and control the disarmed population and raise the tribute exacted in money or kind from the conquered. Sometimes the victorious nation takes possession of the land for itself and distributes it to its own officers and men. In either of these eventualities, however, the old husbandman remains tied to the soil that he used to cultivate and he is forced into a new form of slavery regulated by laws of varying degrees of severity: the new masters must undertake military service and pay tribute as their condition of tenure. In still other cases, the conquering nation reserves for itself the ownership of the land of the conquered and distributes only the usufruct to its captains on these same conditions. Nearly always circumstances compel the conquerors to combine all these three methods of rewarding their soldiers and despoiling their victims.

From this moment we see new classes of men arising: the descendants of the ruling race, and those of the oppressed nation; a hereditary nobility which must not be confused with the patrician class of a republic; a common people condemned to toil, dependence and humiliation without actually being slaves; and, finally, the glebe slaves, as opposed to the domestic slaves, whose less arbitrary servitude enables them to invoke the law against the caprice of their masters.

Here we see the origin of the feudal system, a curse not peculiar to our climate but to be found in nearly every part of the globe at a certain stage of civilization, and in all cases where a single territory has been occupied by two peoples between whom victory in war has established hereditary inequality.

In short, despotism was the fruit of conquest. I mean here by despotism—which I distinguish from transient tyranny —the oppression of a whole nation by a single man who dominates it by opinion, by habit and above all by military force: that is, by an army directly subject to his arbitrary authority but whose prejudices must be respected, whose caprices must be flattered and whose pride and greed must be indulged. Protected by a large, handpicked guard drawn from his own army, attended by the more powerful military captains, controlling his provinces through the services of generals whose word is law to the rank and file of the army, the despot reigns by terror. It is impossible for his oppressed subjects or his scattered generals, themselves often rivals for power, even to conceive the idea of taking arms against him without the certainty of being immediately overwhelmed by the forces at his disposal.

An uprising of the guard or a revolt in the capital can be fatal to a despot, but such events do not shake the institution of despotism itself. The general of a victorious army may destroy a dynasty consecrated by prejudice and establish a new one in its place, but he does so only to exercise the same tyranny himself.

During this third stage, nations who have escaped the misfortune of being either conquerors or conquered show us the simple, hardy virtues of agricultural peoples. They display the morals of heroic times, whose mixture of nobility and savagery, of generosity and barbarism is so attractive that it charms us to the point of admiration and even makes us regret the passing of those times.

But in the empires founded on conquest, we find an entirely different state of morality, exhibiting all the gradations of corruption and debasement into which despotism and superstition can lead the human race. It is there that we see the appearance of taxes on industry and trade, of imposts making the right to employ one's faculties as one wishes something to be bought, of laws restricting one's choice of work and control over one's own property, of laws obliging children to follow their fathers' profession, of confiscations and atrocious tortures—in a word of everything that contempt for the human race has been able to invent in the way of arbitrary acts, legal tyrannies and superstitious atrocities.

[It can be observed that in nations whose history is without great revolutions, the progress of civilization is arrested at a primitive stage: but not before men have felt that need for new ideas and new feelings which is the prime mover in the progress of the human mind, have acquired that taste for the superfluities of luxury which is the spur of industry, and have become infected with that spirit of curiosity which eagerly penetrates the veil nature has drawn across her secrets. But almost everywhere, men, in their desperate efforts to escape from these imperious desires, have pursued and cultivated any physical means of providing themselves with a perpetual supply of new sensations: and in this search they have employed fermented liquors, distilled drinks, opium, tobacco, betel. Some at least of these habits are to be found in almost every nation. They provide pleasures that fill up whole days, or can be enjoyed at any hour, lifting the burden of time from off men's shoulders; pleasures that satisfy the need for distraction and stimulation, and that ultimately dull all desire and prolong the childhood and inactivity of the human mind. These same habits, which have been an obstacle to the progress of ignorant or enslaved peoples, are still, in enlightened countries, obstacles to the diffusion of the pure and equal rays of truth to all classes of men.]

In the first two stages of society, we have seen that some degree of proficiency was achieved in certain crafts, those concerned with work in wood, stone, the bones of animals, the preparing of skins and the making of cloth; in this third stage we shall observe the beginnings of the more difficult arts of dyeing stuffs and making pottery and even a primitive form of metal work.

The progress of these arts would have been slow in isolated nations; but the communications that were established between them, however meagre, accelerated it. A new method, discovered by one people, was imitated by its neighbours. Conquests, which have so often destroyed the arts, in the beginning served to diffuse them and to advance their progress: although later they arrested their growth or contributed to their decline.

[We see several of these arts developed to the highest degree of perfection by peoples amongst whom the degradation of all human faculties has been brought about by the long influence of superstition and despotism. But if we observe even the finest achievements of this servile labour, we find no evidence of genius; their greatest works seem to be the slow and painful result of tedious routine, and we perceive side by side with an industry that astonishes us, traces of ignorance and stupidity which betray its origin.]

In peaceful and sedentary societies, astronomy, medicine, the basic ideas of anatomy, some knowledge of plants and minerals and the first elements of the study of natural phenomena were perfected, or rather attained maturity as a result of the mere passage of time, which increased the fund of observations and gradually led men to perceive almost automatically the general conclusions to be drawn from them.

Yet such progress was extremely uncertain and science might have remained for much longer in its early infancy if certain families, above all if particular castes, had not made use of it as the instrument of their power and glory.

Men had by this stage added the observation of man and society to that of nature. A small number of maxims of practical morality and politics were handed down from generation to generation. Particular castes laid claim to them and monopolized religious ideas, prejudices and superstitions. They were thus the heirs to those primitive groups or families of charlatans and sorcerers; but, to catch shrewder minds, they used subtler means. Such knowledge as they possessed, the seeming asceticism of their lives and their hypocritical disdain for the customary objects of common human desire lent an air of authority to their magic, whilst their magic in turn consecrated in the eyes of the people their exiguous knowledge and their hypocritical virtue. From the beginning the members of these classes pursued two quite different aims with an almost equal enthusiasm; the one being the acquisition of new knowledge, and the other the use of what knowledge they possessed in order to deceive the people and dominate their minds.

Their wise men concentrated above all on astronomy and, as far as we can judge from the scattered remains of the monuments to their work, it seems that they attained the highest degree of knowledge possible without the use of the telescope or higher mathematical theory. Indeed relying on a long series of observations man can arrive at a knowledge of the movements of the stars precise enough to allow him to calculate and predict celestial phenomena. These empirical laws, which are the easier to deduce the longer the period covered by the observations, did not lead these astronomers to the discovery of the general laws of the system of the universe, but they were sufficient to satisfy men's needs, or their curiosity, and to augment the prestige of those who had taken upon themselves the exclusive right to instruct others. It also seems that we are indebted to these men for the ingenious idea of arithmetical scales, the happy discovery of the method of representing all numbers by a small set of signs, and of carrying out by very simple technical operations calculations that would be beyond the powers of our unaided intelligence. This is the first example of those methods which double the power of the human mind and by the aid of which it can advance its frontiers indefinitely.

But we do not find these people developing arithmetic beyond its primitive operations. Their geometry, which contained all that it was useful to know for land-surveyance and astronomy, stopped short at the famous theorem that Pythagoras was later to introduce into Greece or discover anew. They left the theory of their machines to those who had to operate them; however, there are some stories, mixtures of truth and myth, that seem to suggest that they did in fact cultivate this branch of science in order to impress men with prodigies. The laws of motion and rational mechanics were of no interest to them. If they studied pharmacy and surgery and particularly the treatment of wounds, they neglected anatomy. Their botanical knowledge and their knowledge of natural history was limited to substances that could be used as remedies, and certain plants and minerals whose singular properties could serve their ends. Their chemistry, which consisted of a few simple techniques without any theory, method or analysis, was used only for making certain solutions; and they had a few secrets useful in medicine or the arts, and some that

were suitable for producing wonders to dazzle the eyes of
an ignorant multitude led by men no less ignorant than
itself.

The progress of science was for them only a secondary
aim, a means of perpetuating and extending their power.
They sought truth only to spread error, and it is not
strange that they found it so rarely.

However, this progress, slow and uncertain as it was,
would have been impossible if there had not been men who
understood the art of writing, the only method of establishing and maintaining a tradition, of communicating and
transmitting knowledge as it grows. So hieroglyphics must
have been one of their earliest inventions or else existed
before the formation of the teaching castes. As their aim
was not to dispel ignorance but to dominate men, they did
not reveal all their knowledge to the people and what they
did teach them was infected with error. They taught them
not what they believed to be true but what it was in their
own interests for them to know.

They disclosed nothing to them without an admixture of
the supernatural, the holy and the heavenly, as a result of
which they were regarded as superior to common humanity,
clothed with a divine character, having received from heaven
itself knowledge forbidden to other mortals.

They had two doctrines, one for themselves, the other
for the people—and often, as they were divided into several
orders, each of these reserved some mysteries for itself.
All the lower orders were at once scoundrels and dupes,
and this vast system of hypocrisy was known in its entirety
only to a few adepts.

Nothing contributed more to the establishment of this
double doctrine than the changes in language which were
the work of time and of the impact of different tribes upon
one another: for the initiates of the doctrine kept to themselves either their ancient language or that of some foreign
tribe, and so possessed a language understood by them alone.

The earliest form of writing, in which objects were signified by a more or less exact representation either of the object itself or of an analogous object, gave way to a simpler form of writing in which representation was all but eliminated, and in which signs were already used in a purely conventional fashion; in this way the secret doctrine had its written, as it already had its spoken language.

In the infancy of language nearly every word is a metaphor and every phrase an allegory. The mind grasps the figurative and the literal sense simultaneously. The word evokes the idea and at the same time the appropriate image by which the idea is expressed; but after a time the human mind becomes so accustomed to using the word in this figurative sense that by a process of abstraction it tends to fix on this alone and to lose sight of its original meaning: and so the secondary and metaphorical sense of the word gradually becomes its ordinary, normal meaning. The priests, who were the guardians of this original allegorical language, used it in their dealings with the people who were by now incapable of understanding it properly for, having used it so long in one way, they had come to think of this as the only way of doing so; with the result that when the priests used some expression and meant by it a quite simple truth, the people understood by it heaven knows what absurdity. The priests exploited the written word in a similar fashion, for when they used signs to represent some astronomical phenomena or some incident in the cycle of the seasons, the people saw only references to human beings, animals and monsters.

So, for example, the priests in their meditations almost universally developed a metaphysical system based on the idea of a vast eternal Whole: of which all created beings were but parts and of which all observed changes in the universe were so many various modifications. For them the heavens consisted merely of clusters of stars sown in space, of planets describing their various revolutions, and of other

purely physical phenomena the result of the configurations
of these astronomical bodies. The priests gave names to
these constellations and planets and to the fixed and the
moving stars in order to plot their positions and their
motion and to explain them. But their language, their
manner of representing these metaphysical notions, these
scientific truths, whether in the spoken or in the written
word, suggested to the minds of the people the wildest
system of mythology and laid the foundations of the most
absurd beliefs, the most ridiculous rituals, the most shameful
or barbarous practices.

Such is the origin of almost all known religions: which
were subsequently to become encrusted with fresh myths,
the work of the hypocrisy or the extravagance of their
founders and their founders' proselytes.   ·

[These priestly castes gained control of education in
order to train men to suffer more patiently the chains that
had as it were, become identified with their existence, so
that they were now without even the possibility of desiring
to break them. But if we wish to know the lengths to which
these institutions can carry their destructive power over
the human faculties, even without the help of superstitious
terrors, we must, for a moment, turn our attention to
China: for here we have a people who seem to have outstripped all the other nations in the arts and the sciences
only to find themselves overtaken by them all in turn; a
people who, for all their knowledge of artillery, have been
unable to prevent themselves from being conquered by
barbarians; a country where knowledge of the sciences is
open to all and represents the only door to advancement,
and yet where the sciences, being subject to absurd prejudices, are condemned to an eternal mediocrity; and where
even the invention of printing has remained entirely useless
for the progress of the human mind.]

Men whose interest it was to deceive, must soon have
wearied of the search for truth. They were satisfied with

the docility of the people and, they thought they no longer
needed new means of ensuring its continuance. Little by
little they too forgot a part of the truth hidden under their
allegories; they preserved of their old science only what
was strictly necessary if they were to retain the confidence
of their disciples, and they ended by becoming the dupes of
their own myths.

From this moment onwards, all scientific progress was
at an end; even a part of what former centuries had wit-
nessed, was lost to future generations, and the human mind,
given up to ignorance and prejudice, was condemned to
shameful stagnation in those vast empires whose uninterrupted existence has dishonoured Asia for so long.

It is only amongst the inhabitants of this continent that
we can observe such a combination of civilization and
decadence. Among the other nations of the earth we find
either those whose development has been arrested and who
present us with the spectacle of mankind at the time of the
infancy of the human race, or those who have been dragged
forward by the course of events through the later stages of
human development whose history it remains for us to
outline.

At the time that we are considering, these same peoples
of Asia had invented the alphabet and used it instead of
hieroglyphics, after having apparently first used a method
of writing in which a separate conventional sign was
attached to each idea, the only writing known to the Chinese
even to this day. From history and speculation, we can
form some idea of how the change from hieroglyphics to
this as it were intermediate art must have gradually come
about, but there is no means of knowing at all accurately
either in what country or at what time the alphabet was
first used.

This discovery was finally transmitted to the Greeks,
that race which has exercised such a powerful and happy
influence over the progress of humanity, to whom genius

opened all the ways of truth and whom nature had prepared
and fate destined to be the benefactor and guide of every
natiqn in every age, an honour which up to that time no
other people had shared. One alone has since been able to
conceive the hope of presiding over a new revolution in the
destiny of the human race. Nature and the concatenation of
events seem to have agreed amongst themselves to reserve
this glory for her. But let us not seek to penetrate what the
uncertain future still hides from our eyes.

THE FOURTH STAGE

The progress of the human mind in Greece up to the division of the sciences about the time of Alexander the Great

THE Greeks, disgusted with those kings who, styling themselves the children of the gods, dishonoured humanity by their crimes and acts of violence, organized themselves into a number of different republics, of which Lacedæmonia alone recognized hereditary rule. Even here, however, the authority of such rulers was limited by that of the other officers of state and they were as much subject to law as their citizens; and their power was further weakened by the division of royal state between the eldest sons of the two branches of the family of Heraclides.

The inhabitants of Macedonia, Thessaly and Epirus, who were bound to the Greeks by ties of common origin and common language, were ruled over by princes too weak and divided against each other to become the oppressors of Greece but yet strong enough to protect her from Scythian invasions from the north.

In the west, Italy, divided into a number of small and isolated states, could not be any cause of fear to the Greeks. Practically the whole of Sicily and all the magnificent harbours of southern Italy were already occupied by Greek colonies, which while preserving friendly relations with their mother cities, nevertheless formed independent republics. Other colonies had been established on the islands of the Aegean Sea and along one stretch of the coast of Asia Minor. Ultimately the only real threat to the independence of Greece and the freedom of its inhabitants was the prospect of this part of the Asiatic continent joining forces with the vast empire of Cyrus.

Tyranny lasted longer in some of these colonies than in others, notably in those that dated from before the expulsion of the royal families, but still it could nowhere be regarded as anything but a transitory and partial curse making for the unhappiness of the inhabitants of certain towns but having no real effect upon the general spirit of the nation.

Greece had received her arts, some of her science, her religious system and her alphabet from the peoples of the East: the communications established between her and these peoples by means either of exiles from the East who had sought refuge in Greece or of Greeks who travelled in the Orient, brought to Greece the knowledge and the mistakes of Asia and Egypt.

It was impossible in Greece for the sciences to become the occupation and preserve of any one particular caste. The task of the priests was limited to the offices of religion. As a result genius could display itself to the full without submitting to pedantic regulations or to the hypocritical system of a seminary. All men had an equal right to know the truth. All could search for it and disseminate it to all in its entirety.

It was this happy circumstance, even more than the enjoyment of political liberty, that allowed the human mind in Greece an independence which was a sure guarantee of the speed and extent of its future progress.

However the scholars and scientists of Greece, who soon adopted the more modest name of philosopher, or friend of science and knowledge, lost themselves in the immensity of the ambitious scheme that they embraced. They wanted to penetrate the secrets of human and divine nature, of the origin of the world and the origin of the human race: they attempted to reduce the whole of nature to one principle, and all phenomena in the universe to one single law: they

sought to incorporate in one rule of conduct all the obligations of morality and the secret of true happiness. So,
instead of discovering truth, they erected systems: they
neglected the observation of facts for the cultivation of the
imagination, and, unable to submit their opinions to proof,
they tried to defend them by casuistry.

Yet it was these same men who pursued geometry and
astronomy with such success. Greece was indebted to them
for the first principles of these sciences, some of which
they discovered for themselves and some of which they
introduced from the East but introduced them not just as
accepted opinion but as theories whose principles and
proofs they had mastered. Out of the obscurity of these
systems two felicitous ideas shine forth, ideas which will
appear again in more enlightened ages.

Democritus regarded all phenomena of the universe as
the result of the conjunction and movement of simple
bodies of determinate and unchangeable form, and the
universe as having received an initial impulse which
generated a certain force which, though it might vary from
atom to atom, always remains constant throughout the
whole. Pythagoras asserted that the universe was governed
by a harmony whose principles could be discovered by
investigating the properties of numbers; in other words
that all phenomena were subject to general calculable laws.

It is easy to recognize in these two ideas the bold systems
of Descartes and the philosophy of Newton.

Pythagoras further discovered by meditation, or perhaps
learnt from Egyptian or Indian priests, the correct disposition of the heavenly bodies and the true system of the world:
and this he imparted to the Greeks. But this system was too
much at variance with the evidence of the senses and too
opposed to popular notions for the flimsy proofs on which
it rested to carry real conviction. It remained an obscure
doctrine buried in the heart of the Pythagorean school, and
disappeared along with it, to reappear towards the end of

the sixteenth century, supported by sure proofs, which could then triumph over the natural repugnance of the senses and over the still more powerful and dangerous prejudices of superstition.

This Pythagorean school had spread chiefly in Magna Graecia, and there it produced legislators and intrepid champions of the rights of man before it succumbed to the onslaughts of the tyrants. One of them burned the Pythagoreans in their school; and this was doubtless sufficient reason for the survivors to abandon a name which had become too dangerous and to lay aside those methods which served only to arouse the wrath of the enemies of liberty and reason, even if it did not induce them to abjure philosophy and forswear the cause of the people.

One of the essentials for any sound philosophy is to produce for every science an exact and precise language in which every symbol represents some well defined and circumscribed idea; and so by rigorous analysis to guarantee that every idea is well defined and circumscribed.

The Greeks, however, exploited the vices of ordinary language in order to play upon the meanings of words, to confuse the mind with paltry equivocations and to derange it by using the same sign on different occasions to express different ideas. This casuistry at once gave an edge to men's minds and also sapped their strength by involving them in battles against chimerical difficulties. This philosophy of words which attempted to bridge those gulfs before which human reason seemed to be brought to a halt by an obstacle superior to its powers, in no way furthered the immediate progress of the human mind, although it prepared a way for its future advance: an observation that we shall later have occasion to repeat.

It was this attachment to questions that are perhaps for ever insoluble, it was this infatuation with projects solely on the score of their importance or impressiveness with no thought for whether there exists any possible means of fulfilling them, it was this desire to establish theories before assembling facts and to construct the universe before learning how to observe it, that was the error that, though excusable enough, from the very beginning retarded the progress of philosophy. Socrates, in his war against the Sophists, covering with ridicule their vain but subtle arguments, cried out to the Greeks to recall to earth a philosophy which had lost itself in the clouds. He did not despise astronomy or geometry or the observation of natural phenomena nor did he have the wrong and childish idea of confining the human mind to the study of morals alone. On the contrary, it was to his teaching and to that of his disciples that we owe the progress of the mathematical and physical sciences. In the various comedies in which he is ridiculed, the reproach that gives rise to the largest number of quips is that he cultivated geometry, studied meteors, drew maps and made experiments with burning glasses—of whose great age we should indeed be ignorant if it were not for a farce of Aristophanes. All that Socrates wanted to do was to warn men to confine themselves to those things that nature has placed within their reach, to make sure of every step before attempting a new one, and to study what lay around them before embarking for strange and unfamiliar lands.

The death of Socrates is an important event in human history. It was the first crime that marked the beginning of the war between philosophy and superstition, a war which is still being waged amongst us between this same philosophy and the oppressors of humanity and in which the burning of the Pythagorean school was such a significant event. The history of this war will occupy one of the most important places in the picture that it still remains for us to trace.

It was with a heavy heart that the priests observed how mankind in its efforts to perfect its own powers of reasoning and to trace everything back to origins, discovered the full absurdity of their dogmas, the full extravagance of their ceremonies, the full imposture of their oracles and miracles. They were afraid that these philosophers would unmask them before the pupils who attended their schools; that such knowledge would then be transmitted to anyone who, in pursuit of authority or prestige for himself, felt the necessity to cultivate his mind; that as a result priestly dominion would soon hold sway only over the most vulgar of the people, and that in the end even they would be undeceived. Hypocrisy in terror hastened to accuse the philosophers of impiety towards the gods so that they would be unable to teach the people that these gods were the work of the priests. The philosophers thought to escape persecution by adopting, like the priests, the use of a double doctrine, whereby they confided only to tried and trusted disciples opinions that would too openly offend popular prejudice.

But the priests presented even the simplest physical truths to the people as blasphemies. They persecuted Anaxagoras for having dared to say that the sun was bigger than the Peloponnese. Socrates could not escape their onslaught, for by this time there was no Pericles left in Athens to come to the defence of genius and virtue. And, besides, Socrates was truly guilty. His hatred of the Sophists and his zeal in recalling errant philosophy to more useful occupations showed the priests that truth alone was the object of his search and that, far from desiring to impose a new system upon mankind and to subject its imagination to his own, he wished only to teach them how to think for themselves. And of all crimes it is this that priestly arrogance knows least how to forgive.

It was at the foot of Socrates' tomb that Plato imparted the lessons that he had learnt from his master.

His delightful style, his brilliant imagination, his pleasant or dignified imagery, the little touches, deft and lively, that in his Dialogues banish all dryness from philosophical discussion, allied to the maxims of a pure and gentle morality which he disseminates there, and the wit with which he makes his people act always in character—all these felicities which time and changing belief have not withered must doubtless have interceded for those philosophic dreams which too often form the basis of his work and for the abuse of words with which his master had so often reproached the Sophists and from which he had been powerless to preserve the greatest of his disciples.

When we read his Dialogues, it seems astonishing that they are the work of a philosopher who in an inscription over the door of his school forbade anyone who had not studied geometry to enter there, and that the man who introduces so boldly such barren and frivolous hypotheses was the founder of a sect in which for the first time the principles of human knowledge were subjected to rigorous examination, so rigorous indeed that some that would be respected by a more enlightened reason were ruthlessly rejected.

But the contradiction disappears when we remember that Plato never speaks in his own name; that his master Socrates always expresses himself with the modesty of doubt; that the various systems are presented in the names of those who were, or were believed by Plato to be, their authors; that these same Dialogues are also a seminary for Pyrrhonism; and that Plato reveals at once the bold imagination of a learned man who likes to construct and elaborate brilliant hypotheses, and the reserve of a philosopher who gives rein to his imagination without allowing himself to be completely carried away by it, since his reason, fortified by salutary doubt, is well able to defend itself against even the most seductive flights of fancy.

The various schools where the doctrine and more particularly the principles and methods of an original thinker were perpetuated—though never to the point of regarding him with docile servility—served the further purpose of uniting in bonds of free brotherhood men engaged in penetrating the secrets of nature. If the master's own opinions too often enjoyed an authority that properly belongs to reason alone and if in this way the institution retarded the progress of knowledge, it also served to diffuse its findings more quickly and over a greater area than would otherwise have been possible at a time when printing was unknown and manuscripts extremely scarce; these great schools whose fame attracted pupils from every part of Greece were the most powerful means of engendering a taste for philosophy and of propagating new truths.

In their rivalry they fought each other with the animosity of sectarianism, and often the interests of truth were sacrificed to the success of some particular doctrine in which the pride of every member of the sect was involved. The selfish desire to win converts corrupted the nobler desire of leading men to the truth. And yet this rivalry was also useful in that it kept men's minds active. The mere spectacle of such disputes and the interest aroused by these intellectual battles introduced a large number of people to the study of philosophy whom the mere love of truth would never have enticed away from business, or pleasure, or perhaps mere idleness.

Since these schools and sects, which the Greeks had the sense never to introduce into public life, remained entirely free, and since anyone could at will open a new school or form a new sect, there was no fear of that enslavement of reason which has been such an insurmountable obstacle to the progress of the human spirit in most other countries.

We shall show what influence these philosophers exercised over the thought of Greece, her morals, laws and government; and how this influence arose largely because they never had nor wanted to play any part in political life, because, whatever sect they belonged to, they made the voluntary withdrawal from public affairs a maxim of conduct, because they affected to distinguish themselves from other men as much by their lives as by their opinions.

As we trace the picture of these different sects, we shall be occupied less with their systems than with the principles of their philosophy, less in looking for an exact knowledge of the various absurd doctrines which are anyhow too often hidden from us by a language that has become almost unintelligible, and more in showing what general mistakes led them astray and in discovering their origin in the natural progress of the human mind.

We shall concern ourselves especially with an analysis of the applied sciences and the gradual perfection of their methods.

·At this period philosophy cast its net over all the sciences except medicine, which had already become a separate study. The writings of Hippocrates will show us what was the existing state of that science and of those sciences with which it was naturally connected but which had at this time no independent existence of their own. The mathematical sciences had been successfully cultivated in the schools of Thales and Pythagoras. Nevertheless they had not progressed far beyond the point that they had reached in the seminaries of the East. But after the founding of the Platonic school they broke down the barrier that had been imposed by the attempts to limit them to immediate and practical uses. This philosopher was the first to solve the problem of the duplication of the cube by a mechanical construction, an ingenious method, and one of great rigour. His early disciples discovered conic sections and determined their more important properties: and in doing so, they opened up an immense horizon to genius towards which it will be able to struggle forward until the end of all time, but which will recede from it with every step that it takes forward.

The progress of the political sciences in ancient Greece is not to be attributed entirely to philosophy. In those small republics, so jealous of their freedom and their independence, there was an almost universal assent to the idea of conferring on one man alone, not the power to make laws but the task of formulating them and presenting them to the people who would scrutinize and sanction them.

E

[Thus the people imposed work on the philosopher when his virtues or wisdom had gained their confidence, but they did not endow him with any authority. He exercised alone and by himself what has come to be called the legislative power. The baneful custom of using] superstition as a prop for political institutions has too often sullied the execution of a scheme so well calculated to give the laws of any country the systematic unity they need if they are to be readily and smoothly executed and to prove enduring. However, politics did not yet possess sufficiently constant principles for people not to be afraid of seeing the legislators introduce their prejudices and passions into the practice of law-making.

For at that time the legislator did not think it his task to set up a society of free and equal men, based on reason, on the rights that all men have received in equal degree from nature, and on the maxims of universal justice; he thought that he had discharged his duty when he had made laws that would allow the members of a hereditary society to preserve their freedom, to live without fear of injustice and to defend themselves against any external threat to their independence.

As it was assumed that laws, which were nearly always tied to religion and consecrated by oaths, would last for ever, less interest was taken in providing a country with the means of peaceful reform than in preventing the alteration of fundamental laws, and in ensuring that changes in detail would not debase the system nor corrupt its essence. People looked for institutions that would exalt and encourage love of one's country, and this was taken to include love of its laws and even of its customs: they looked for some way of organizing the powers within the state that would ensure the execution of the law against the indifference or corruption of the magistrates, the influence of powerful citizens and the turbulence of the masses.

The rich who alone were in a position to acquire knowledge, could seize power and oppress the poor, and so force them into the arms of a tyrant. The ignorance and fickleness of the common people and their jealousy of powerful citizens could provide these latter with both the desire and the means to establish an aristocratic despotism or to deliver the enfeebled State to the ambitions of its neighbours. Forced to preserve themselves at one and the same time from these two dangers, the Greek lawgivers had recourse to a variety of devices, some more, some less fortunate in their outcome but all of them imbued with that subtlety, with that wisdom from now onwards so characteristic of the general spirit of the nation.

There is hardly to be found in any modern republic or in any of those schemes devised by philosophers an institution of which the Greek republics did not provide the model or supply an example. So the Amphictionic league and the confederacies of the Etolians, the Arcadians, and the Acheans show us federal constitutions of a more or less closely knit type: and amongst the various races who were linked by ties of common descent and language, and similar habits, opinions and religious beliefs, there were established a less primitive law of nations and more liberal rules of trade.

[The mutual relations between agriculture, industry and trade and the constitution of the state and its legislation, and their influence over its prosperity, its power and its liberty could not escape the attention of a clever active people who busied themselves with matters of public interest: and so we observe the rudiments of that comprehensive and useful art, known today as political economy.]

Mere observation of actual governments was enough to make politics into quite an extensive science. [And so even in the writings of the philosophers it appears more as a science of facts, as, so to say, an empirical science, than as a genuine theory founded on general principles which are drawn from nature and acknowledged by reason. This is the point of view from which the political ideas of Aristotle and Plato can most satisfactorily be considered if we are to understand them aright and appreciate them to the full.]

Nearly all the institutions of the Greeks assume the existence of slavery and also the feasibility of bringing together the whole body of citizens in one public place. If we are to judge of the practical value of these institutions and, above all, to assess their relevance to the great nations of the modern age, we must not for a moment lose sight of these two important differences. We cannot, however, reflect upon the former without the painful thought that even the most perfect arrangements then known had as their object the liberty or the happiness of at most only half of the human race.

[For the Greeks education was an important part of politics. It formed men much more for their country than for themselves or for their family. This principle cannot be adopted for any but small populations where there is better justification for assuming the existence of a national interest that is different from the interests of the whole of humanity. It is practicable only in countries where the really hard work in agriculture and in the arts and crafts is carried out by slaves. This education was virtually limited to physical exercises, the principles of morality and the habits proper to arousing a jealous patriotism: everything else could be learnt without restriction in the schools of philosophers or rhetoricians and in the studios of artists— and this liberty is yet another cause of the superiority of the Greeks.]

In their politics as in their philosophy we can discover a general principle to which history provides only a very small number of exceptions. This is the habit of seeing law not so much as an instrument for removing the causes of evil as a means of eradicating its effects by playing those causes off one against another; the practice, in government, of turning prejudices and vices to good account rather than trying to dispel or repress them; a greater interest in depriving man of his true nature, in exalting and inflaming his imagination than in perfecting and purifying those inclinations and predilections which are the necessary product of his moral constitution—all these mistakes arising from the more general mistake of identifying the natural man with the product of the existing state of civilization, with, that is, man corrupted by prejudices, artificial passions and social customs.

This observation is all the more important, and the mistake is one whose origin it is even more necessary to trace so that we may eradicate it effectively, since it has been transmitted down to our own age, and since it still only too often corrupts our morality and our politics.

[If we compare the legislation, and especially the form and the rules of judgment in Greece with those existing amongst Eastern races, we shall see that with the latter laws were a yoke under which people were bound into slavery whereas with the former they were the conditions of a common pact between man and man; for the former the purpose of legal forms was that the will of the master should be accomplished, for the latter that the freedom of the citizens should not be crushed; with the one, laws were made for the benefit of him who imposed them, with the others, for the benefit of him who had to submit to them; with the one, people were made to fear the law, with the others, they were taught to respect it. These differences we shall find persisting into the modern age, and separating the laws of free peoples from the laws of slave populations. And, finally, we shall see that in Greece, man had at least a feeling for his rights even if he was not as yet fully cognizant of them, not as yet able to fathom their nature, range and full extent.]

At this stage, marked for the Greeks by the dawn of philosophy, and the first advances in the sciences, the fine arts attained a degree of perfection that no other people had known before and that scarcely any has since achieved.

Homer lived at the time of the dissensions that accompanied the fall of tyrants and the formation of republics. Sophocles, Euripides, Pindar, Thucydides, Demosthenes, Phidias and Apelles were contemporaries of Socrates or Plato.

We shall sketch the progress of these arts and discuss its cause, distinguishing between what can be seen as the perfection of art itself and what is due only to the happy genius of the artist, a distinction which should remove the narrow limits that have been set to the process of perfection in the fine arts. We shall show the influence that forms of government, systems of law and the spirit of religious worship exercised over their progress, and we shall try to discover how much they owed to philosophy and how much philosophy owed to them.

We shall reveal how liberty, the arts and enlightenment have helped towards the softening and improvement of manners; how the vices of the Greeks, which are so often attributed to the very progress of their civilization, were those of a coarser age; and how enlightenment and the cultivation of the arts tempered them when they could not destroy them utterly. We shall prove that the eloquent declamations made against the arts and sciences are founded upon a mistaken application of history, and that, on the contrary, the progress of virtue has always gone hand in hand with that of enlightenment, just as the progress of corruption has always followed, or heralded, its decadence.

THE FIFTH STAGE

The progress of the sciences from their division to their decline

It was in Plato's lifetime that his pupil Aristotle opened a rival school of his own in Athens itself.

Not only did he include all the sciences in his teaching, but he also applied philosophical method to poetry and rhetoric. He was the first man with the courage and imagination to see that this method could be applied to everything attainable by human intelligence, since human intelligence, always using the same faculties, must always be subject to the same laws. As the scope of his plan increased, the greater need did he feel to separate its various provinces and to determine more precisely the frontiers of each. After him most philosophers, even entire schools of philosophy, have restricted themselves to one or other of these provinces.

The mathematical and physical sciences formed one large division by themselves. As they are based on calculation and observation and as their findings are indifferent in just those matters on which the various sects were divided, they became separated from philosophy, over which the various sects still reigned. They became the preserve of learned men who were almost without exception wise enough not to embroil themselves in the disputes between the various schools, disputes in which everyone competed only for fame and which were better calculated to promote the transient renown of particular philosophers than to contribute to the progress of philosophy itself. The word

philosophy soon came to signify only the general principles
governing the world order, metaphysics, dialectic and the
moral sciences of which politics was a part. Fortunately
this division preceded the time when Greece after long
struggles lost her liberty.

The sciences found a refuge in the capital of Egypt, which
the despotic rulers of that city would perhaps have refused
to philosophy. Princes who derived a large proportion of
their wealth and power from the traffic which stretched
from the Mediterranean to the Asiatic Ocean, were anxious
to encourage those sciences which were useful for navigation and commerce. These sciences thus escaped that more
rapid process of decline that overtook philosophy, whose
splendour faded with the disappearance of liberty. The
despotism of the Romans, a people who were indifferent to
the progress of knowledge, did not reach Egypt until very
late, by which time Alexandria had become necessary for
Rome's survival. Since this town was already as much the
metropolis of the sciences as it was the capital of commerce,
it was by itself able to safeguard that sacred flame; the size
of its population, its wealth, the great influx of strangers,
and the establishments founded by the Ptolemies, which the
conquerors saw no reason to destroy, were enough to assure
it the power to do so.

The Academic sect in which, from the earliest days,
mathematics had been cultivated and which virtually confined its philosophical teaching to proving the utility of
doubt and indicating the narrow limits of certainty, became
the sect of scholars: and, as this doctrine could not alarm
the despots, it dominated the school of Alexandria.

The theory of conic sections and the method of using
them in the construction of geometric loci or in the solution
of problems, and the discovery of some other curves, extended the scope of geometry, which had hitherto been
narrow. Archimedes discovered the quadrature of the
parabola and calculated the surface of the sphere, and these

were the first steps in that theory of limits which determines the ultimate value of a quantity or the value that the quantity ever approaches but never reaches, and in the science that teaches us how to find the ratios of vanishing quantities and how to progress from the knowledge of these ratios to determine those of finite magnitudes; in the calculation, in short, to which the moderns have, with more vanity than accuracy, given the name of infinitesimal calculus. Archimedes was the first to determine the ratio between the diameter of a circle and its circumference and to show how to obtain values for it approximating closer and closer to the true one; he also discovered the method of approximation, a happy contribution to the small stock of known methods and to the meagre condition of the science itself.

We can consider him in some measure the creator of rational mechanics. We are indebted to him for the theory of the lever and the discovery of the principle of hydrostatics according to which the weight of a body placed in a liquid is reduced by an amount equal to the weight of the mass that it has displaced.

The screw that is named after him, his burning-mirrors, his remarkable inventions during the siege of Syracuse attest to his skill in mechanics, a science which had been totally ignored because it had never proved possible to put it to any practical use. These great discoveries, these new sciences place Archimedes amongst those happy men of genius whose lives are landmarks in the history of mankind and whose existence seems to be a generous gift of nature.

We find the beginnings of algebra in the school of Alexandria; that is to say, we find the calculation of magnitudes considered simply as such. The nature of the problems set and solved in the book of Diophantus required that numbers should be regarded as having a general value which was indeterminate and subject only to certain conditions. But this science had not then, as it has today, its own symbols and correct methods and technical operations. General values were designated by words and the solutions to problems were discovered and developed only by a long chain of reasoning.

Certain observations made by the Chaldeans were sent back to Aristotle by Alexander and these gave an impetus to the progress of astronomy. The most remarkable achievements in this field were due to the genius of Hipparchus. If, after him in astronomy, as after Archimedes in geometry and mechanics, there were no discoveries, no contributions that changed, as it were, the whole face of the science, both continued to perfect themselves for a long while, to expand and to be supplemented by a great deal of detailed research.

In his history of animals Aristotle had formulated the principles and given an invaluable model of the correct way of making precise observations and systematic descriptions of natural objects, and the method of classifying observations and drawing general conclusions from them.

Plant and mineral history were studied on the lines that he had laid down but with less precision and from a narrower and less philosophical point of view. The progress of anatomy was very slow, not only because religious prejudices were opposed to the dissection of corpses but because popular opinion regarded contact with them as a kind of moral defilement.

The medicine of Hippocrates was a mere science of observation, which had so far led to nothing but purely empirical methods. The spirit of sectarianism and a taste for hypotheses soon infected the doctors, but if their mistakes were more numerous than their discoveries, if their prejudices or systems did more harm than their observations did good, it is not to be denied that during this period medicine made some real progress, small though it was.

Aristotle did not carry into physics either the exactitude or the wise caution that characterize his history of animals. He paid tribute to the customs of his age and to the spirit of the schools, in disfiguring physics with those hypothetical principles which in their vague generality explain everything with facility because they can explain nothing with precision.

Moreover, observation by itself is not enough; what is necessary is to experiment, and this in turn requires instruments. It seems as though not enough facts had been collected and as though those that had been collected had not been examined in enough detail, for there to be any felt need, any idea of this method of asking questions of nature and forcing her to answer them. At this period, therefore, the history of the progress of physics has nothing to show except the amassing of a small number of known facts, all due to chance or to observations made in the exercise of the various arts rather than to the research of scientists. Hydraulics and especially optics yielded a somewhat less sterile harvest but even here it was more a case of the compilation of observed facts, observed because they forced themselves on man's attention, than of theories or physical laws discovered by experiment or arrived at through meditation.

[Agriculture had not gone beyond matters of simple routine and a few rules which the priests transmitted to the people, and in doing so, corrupted by superstition. It became an important and respected art with the Greeks and even more with the Romans, an art whose rules and precepts were matters of great interest even to the most learned men. These anthologies of observations, set out with some precision and gathered with some discernment, were able to enlighten practice and diffuse useful methods, but men were still a long way away from the age of experiment and of mathematical observation.]

The mechanical arts came to be connected with the sciences; philosophers examined the various processes, tried to discover their origin, studied their history and aimed at producing an account of the methods and achievements in this field in different countries, at collating them and handing them down to posterity.

So we see Pliny including man, nature and the arts in the huge plan of his Natural History, an invaluable inventory of all the existing riches of the human mind. Pliny's claim to our gratitude is not affected by the reproach that can justifiably be brought against him, that he accepted with too little discrimination and too much incredulity anything that the ignorance or lying vanity of chroniclers and travellers offered up to his insatiable greed for omniscience.

With the decadence of Greece, Athens, who in the days of her power had honoured letters and philosophy, was now in her turn indebted to them for her capacity to preserve a little longer some vestiges of her ancient glory. It was no longer at her tribune that the destinies of Greece and Asia were weighed; but it was in her Schools that the Romans learnt the secrets of eloquence; and it was at the foot of Demosthenes' lamp that the first of the Roman orators was formed.

The Academy, the Lyceum, the Stoa and the gardens of Epicurus were the cradle and the principal school of the four sects that disputed the empire of philosophy.

In the Academy it was taught that nothing is certain ; that in no matter can man attain true certainty or even perfect understanding; finally—and it is difficult to go further—that he cannot even be sure of the impossibility of knowing anything, and that he must doubt even the necessity of doubting everything. The opinions of other philosophers were expounded and defended and disputed here, but merely as so many hypotheses proper for exercising the mind and for impressing on man, by the uncertainty that always attended these disputes, the vanity of human knowledge and the absurdity of the dogmatic confidence of other sects.

But this method of doubt which reason sanctions as long as it encourages us merely to avoid arguments about words to which we can attach no clear and precise ideas, to proportion our belief in a proposition to its degree of probability, and to determine for the various species of know-

ledge the limits of certainty to which we can attain—this
form of doubt, if it extends to ascertained truth, if it attacks
the principles of morality, becomes either stupidity or mad-
ness, it favours ignorance and corruption, and it is to these
lengths that the Sophists went who succeeded the first
disciples of Plato in the Academy.

We shall describe the progress of these sceptics and the
cause of their errors; we shall try to discover how much of
what is exaggerated in their doctrine should be attributed
to their passion for attracting attention to themselves by
holding grotesque opinions; we shall notice that however
adequately they may be refuted by the instincts of the rest
of humanity and by the principles whereby they regulated
the conduct of their own lives, they were never either
properly understood or properly refuted by philosophers.

However, this exaggerated scepticism did not carry with
it the whole of the Academy. On the contrary the doctrine
which was drawn from Plato's Dialogues, that there is an
eternal idea of the just, the beautiful and the virtuous, independent of the interests of men, of their conventions, even
of their existence, an idea, which, once it is imprinted in the
soul, becomes for us the principle of duty and the rule of
conduct, continued to be expounded in his school, and
served as a foundation for the teaching of morality.

Aristotle understood no better than his masters the art
of analysing ideas; that is to say the art of working back
stage by stage to these simple ideas out of which more
complex ideas are formed by the process of combination, of
tracing the origin of these simple ideas, and so of following
the progress of the mind and the development of its
faculties. His metaphysic therefore was like that of other
philosophers, only a vague doctrine, founded at times on an
abuse of words, at times on mere hypotheses. Even so we
owe him the important truth, the first step in the science
of the human mind, that *even our most abstract, as it were
our most purely intellectual, ideas have their origin in our*

sensations. He did not, however, develop this discovery. It was more the insight of a man of genius than the result of a series of observations analysed with precision and combined to bring forth a general truth. And so it required another twenty centuries before this seed, thrown on barren ground, bore useful fruit.

In his logic Aristotle reduced all proofs to a series of arguments cast in a syllogistic form; he further divided all propositions into four exhaustive classes; he learnt how to identify out of all the possible combinations of propositions of these four classes taken in threes, those which correspond to valid syllogisms and do so necessarily; in this way, we can judge the soundness or viciousness of an argument merely by knowing to which combination it belongs. The art of correct reasoning is thus somehow dependent on technical rules.

This ingenious notion has remained useless up to the present time; but perhaps it may one day be used as the first step towards that perfection which the art of reasoning and dispute seems still to achieve.

According to Aristotle every virtue occupies a position between two vices of which the one is its total absence, the other its excess. Each virtue is therefore merely one of our natural inclinations, which nature forbids us either to resist or to obey too fervently. This general principle may have been suggested to him by one of those vague ideas of order and conformity which were so common in philosophy at that time; but he verified it by an appeal to the vocabulary actually used by the Greeks to describe the virtues.

About the same time two new sects, which made morality dependent on two at least apparently opposed principles, competed for men's allegiance: they exerted an influence far beyond the limits of the Schools, and hastened the downfall of Greek superstition, only unfortunately for it to be replaced by another superstition, gloomier, more pernicious, a bitterer enemy to enlightenment.

The Stoics saw virtue and happiness as consisting in the possession of a soul that was equally insensible to joy and pain, that was freed from every passion, that was superior to all fears and weaknesses and that knew no true good but virtue and no real evil but remorse. They believed that Man had the power to raise himself to this height if he had a strong and inflexible will to do so, and that then, independent of fate, always master of himself, he would be equally impervious to vice and misery. One spirit animates the world and is everywhere present—if indeed it be not all things itself, if anything at all exist apart from it. Human souls are emanations of it. The soul of the wise man, which has not sullied its original purity, is, at the moment of death, reunited with this universal spirit. Death would thus be good, were it not that the wise man who follows nature, who is hardened against all that the vulgar call evils, finds even greater dignity in regarding it as something indifferent.

Epicurus regarded happiness as the enjoyment of pleasure and the absence of pain. Virtue consists in following one's natural inclinations albeit knowing how to purify them and direct them. Temperance, whereby we prevent pain and preserve our natural faculties at their full strength and so secure for ourselves all the enjoyment prepared for us by nature; abstention from violent or discordant passions which torment and lacerate the heart once it is given over to their bitter and angry sway; the cultivation, instead, of the gentle and tender affections, indulgence in the pleasures of benevolence; and the preservation of the purity of one's soul so as to avoid shame and remorse which are the punishment of crime, so as to enjoy the delightful feeling that is the reward of good deeds—this is the road that leads to both happiness and virtue.

Epicurus saw the universe as a mere collection of atoms of which the various conjunctions are subject to necessary laws. The human soul itself is one of these conjunctions.

The atoms of which it is composed are united the moment the body begins to live and are dispersed the instant that it dies, to be merged again into the common mass, and ultimately to enter into new conjunctions. Not wishing to offend popular prejudice too directly, Epicurus admitted the gods into his universe, but his gods, indifferent to all human actions, unconcerned with the order of the universe, and subject like other beings to the general laws of its mechanism, were somehow a mere appendage to this system.

The hard, the proud and the unjust sheltered behind the mask of stoicism; sybarites and debauchees often insinuated themselves into the gardens of Epicurus. People calumnied Epicurean principles, accusing them of setting up crude sensual pleasures as the supreme good: and they ridiculed the claims of the sage Zeno who, a slave, racked by gout, turning the millstone, was nevertheless happy, free, and sovereign.

The philosophy that claimed to rise above nature and that which wished only to obey her, the morality that recognized no other good but virtue and that which placed happiness in pleasure, led to the same practical consequences, although they set out from such contrary principles and used such different language. This resemblance between the moral precepts of all religions and all philosophical sects suffices to prove that their truth is something independent of the dogmas of these various religions and the principles of these different sects; that it is to the moral constitution of man that we must look for the foundations of his duties and the origins of his ideas of justice and virtue: a truth to which the Epicureans were closer than any other sect, and it is perhaps for this reason more than any other that they drew down on themselves the hatred of hypocrites of all classes for whom morality is but an object of trade whose monopoly they contest.

The fall of the Greek city-states brought about that of

the political sciences. After Plato, Aristotle and Xenophon, they almost ceased to be included in philosophical systems.

But it is now time to speak of an event which changed the fate of a great part of the world and exerted an influence over the progress of the human mind which has lasted to our own day.

Except for India and China, Rome had extended her dominion over all the nations where the human mind had emerged from the helplessness of its early infancy. She gave laws to all countries where the Greeks had taken their language, their sciences and their philosophy. All these nations tied by chains of defeat to the foot of the Capitol, existed only at the will of Rome and for the passions of her leaders.

[A true picture of the constitution of this powerful city would not be alien to the purpose of this book. We shall see the beginning of the hereditary patriciate and the ingenious arrangements that were used to give it greater stability and strength by rendering it less odious; we shall see a people skilful in the use of arms but employing them hardly ever in domestic quarrels, combining real strength with lawful authority and yet scarcely defending themselves against a proud Senate, who chained them by superstition and dazzled them by the brilliance of its victories; a great nation, the plaything in turn of its tyrants and of its champions, and for four centuries the patient dupe of a system of voting which was absurd, but sacrosanct.]

[We shall see this constitution which was made for a single town, change its nature without changing its form when it was necessary to extend it over a great empire; how, able to maintain itself only by continual warfare, it was soon destroyed by its own armies; and how in the end the sovereign-people, degraded by the habit of being fed at the public expense and corrupted by the largesse of the senators, sold to one man the illusory remains of its useless freedom.]

F

The ambition of the Romans led them to turn to Greece for masters in rhetoric, for with them this art was one of the roads to fortune. That taste for rare and refined enjoyment, that desire for new pleasures, which is born of wealth and idleness, made them aspire to the arts of the Greeks and even the conversation of their philosophers. But philosophy, the sciences, the graphic arts were always plants foreign to Roman soil. The greed of the victors filled Italy with the masterpieces of Greece, looted from the temples and the cities which they adorned and from the peoples whom they consoled in their slavery; but they never dared set up the work of any Roman beside them. Cicero, Lucretius and Seneca wrote eloquently on philosophy in their own language, but the philosophy was Greek; and in order to reform the barbaric calendar of Numa, Cæsar was obliged to employ a mathematician from Alexandria.

Rome, rent for so long by the factions of ambitious generals, embroiled in new campaigns of conquest or agitated by civil discord, at last fell from a state of restless freedom into an even stormier one of military despotism. What place then could the tranquil reflections of philosophy or the sciences find amongst captains who aspired to tyranny, or, a little later, under despots who feared the truth and hated ability and virtue alike? Moreover, philosophy and the sciences are necessarily neglected in all countries where there is an honourable occupation leading to wealth and position that is open to anyone who has a natural inclination for study; and such in Rome was the career of the law.

When, as in the East, laws are tied to religion, the right to interpret them becomes one of the strongest bulwarks of priestly tyranny. In Greece they had been enshrined in the code that was given to each town by its lawgiver; they had been linked to the spirit of the constitution and the established government. They underwent few changes. Often the magistrates abused them; particular injustices were frequent; but the vices of the laws never led to a regular

and coldly calculated system of brigandage. In Rome, where
no other authority than tradition and custom had been
known for a long period of time; where each year the judges
announced the principles on which they would decide all
cases for the period of their magistrature; where the first
written laws were merely a compilation of Greek laws,
edited by the decemvirs, men more concerned to retain their
power than to honour it in the form of sound legislation;
where, in the period in question, laws, dictated alternately
by the Senate and by the people, followed on each other
in rapid succession and all the time were being rescinded
or confirmed, improved or worsened by new declarations, it was not long before the multiplicity, complexity
and obscurity of the laws, the necessary result of a fluid
language, made the study and knowledge of them a science
apart. The Senate, profiting from the popular respect for
ancient institutions, soon felt that the privilege of interpreting the laws was almost equal to the right of making
new ones, and so packed itself with legal experts. The
power of this group outstripped that of the Senate itself;
it grew and grew under the Emperors and became ever
greater as the laws became more fanciful and inchoate.

Jurisprudence is then the only new science that we owe
to the Romans. We intend to trace its history, since it is
relevant to the progress of the science of legislation amongst
the Moderns, and, more particularly, to the obstacles in
the way of this progress.

We shall show how the Romans' respect for positive law
helped in the beginning to keep alive some notion of the
natural rights of man, but later worked against the growth
and propagation of these same ideas: and how we owe to
Roman law a small number of useful truths but a greater
number of tyrannical prejudices.

[The mildness of penal laws under the Republic deserves
our scrutiny. In some measure they made the life of a
Roman citizen sacrosanct. The death penalty could not be

imposed upon him without invoking those extraordinary powers which otherwise presaged public calamities and the fatherland in danger. The entire people could be called upon to judge between one man and the republic. The Romans realized that with a free people temperance of this kind was the only way to prevent the degeneration of political dissension into bloody massacre; they wished to correct by the humanity of the law the ferocious manners of the populace—a populace which even in its games spilt the blood of slaves—and as a result, up to the time of the Gracchi, there is no country that offers us the same spectacle of endless violent disturbances at such little cost in the way of crime and bloodshed.]

[No Roman work on politics has come down to us. That of Cicero on the laws was really nothing but an embellished series of extracts from certain Greek writings. Social science could not have made a home for itself nor have been perfected amongst the convulsions of dying liberty. Under the despotism of the Cæsars its study would have seemed only a conspiracy against their power. Nothing indeed better proves how unknown it was to the Romans than the situation, still unique in history, of an uninterrupted succession of five emperors, from Nerva to Marcus Aurelius, all uniting virtue, talent, enlightenment, love of glory and a zeal for the public good, without one of them instigating one single institution expressive of any desire to curb despotism or prevent revolution or weld together by new ties the various parts of that huge mass whose imminent dissolution was everywhere apparent.]

The union of so many peoples under one domination, and the spread of two languages which divided the Empire, both of which were familiar to nearly all educated men, must both have contributed to produce a more general diffusion of knowledge. Their natural effect was to weaken little by little the differences that separated the philosophical sects, and to unite them in one which would select, out of the various opinions of each, those which conformed most closely to reason, those which reflection and examination had confirmed. Reason must have led philosophers to this conclusion when the effect of time upon sectarian enthusiasm had allowed her voice to be universally heard. So we find already in Seneca some traces of this philosophy; it was never alien to the academic sect, which in the end was identified almost entirely with it; and the last disciples of Plato were the founders of eclecticism.

Almost all the religions of the Empire had been national. But they had also had important features in common and to some degree a family resemblance. These common features were the absence of any metaphysical dogma; a number of fantastic ceremonies which had a meaning incomprehensible to the people and often to the priests themselves; an absurd mythology in which the populace saw only the marvellous history of its gods but which more educated men suspected to be an allegorical representation of more enlightened beliefs; bloody sacrifices; idols which represented the gods and some of which, consecrated by age, were credited with heavenly virtue; pontiffs, each devoted to the cult of a particular divinity, forming no body politic nor even united in a religious community; oracles attached to particular temples and particular statues; and finally, mysteries which their hierophants communicated only after imposing the vow of inviolable secrecy.

We must further mention that the priests, who were arbiters in all matters of religious conscience, had never dared claim to be arbiters in matters of morals, that they directed the offices of worship and not the actions of private life. They sold oracles and auguries to political powers; they could hurl people into wars, or order them to commit crimes; but they exercised no influence over government or laws.

In an empire where the various subject nations had habitual converse with each other and where knowledge everywhere made more or less equal progress, men of education soon perceived that all these forms of worship appertained to one god of whom the countless divinities, the direct objects of popular devotion, were merely the various modifications or intermediaries.

With the Gauls, however, and in some Eastern provinces, the Romans found religions of a different character. There the priests were arbiters of morality, and virtue consisted in obeying the will of a God of whom they claimed to be the sole interpreters. Their dominion embraced the whole man; temple and state were confused; a man was an adorer of Jehovah and Œsus before he was a citizen or a subject of the empire; and the priests decided which human laws their god allowed them to obey.

These religions must have wounded the vanity of the masters of the world. That of the Gauls was too powerful for them not to achieve its immediate destruction. The Jewish nation was even scattered, but the government, either out of disdain or impotence, never extended its vigilance to the obscure sects which were formed soon afterwards out of the ruins of these ancient religions.

One of the advantages of the propagation of Greek philosophy had been the destruction of the belief in popular divinities in all classes that had received any education. A vague theism, or the pure mechanism of Epicurus, was, even in Cicero's day, the ordinary belief of anyone who had cultivated his mind and of all those who directed public affairs. This latter class naturally supported the old religion, but sought to refine it because the great number of gods in every country had tired even the credulity of the people. So we see philosophers building systems upon intermediary spirits, and subjecting themselves to preparations, practices, a religious discipline, in order to make themselves worthier to approach these intelligences superior to man: and it was in the Dialogues of Plato that they sought a foundation for this doctrine.

The people of conquered nations, the misfortuned, and

men of a wretched and inflamed imagination chose to
attach themselves to priestly religions because the priests
who controlled them, in their own interest breathed into
them a belief in equality even in slavery, in the renunciation
of worldly goods and in the existence of heavenly rewards
for the blindly submissive, for the suffering, for those who
had voluntarily humiliated themselves or endured humiliation patiently: a doctrine so seductive in the eyes of
oppressed humanity! However, these priests saw the
necessity of refining their coarse mythology with some
philosophical subtlety, and once again they had recourse to
Plato. His Dialogues were the arsenal to which the two
parties resorted to forge their theological arms. We shall
observe how at a later date Aristotle was honoured in a
similar fashion, and found himself at once the master of the
theologians and the leader of the atheists.

Twenty Egyptian and Jewish sects who were united
against the imperial religion but fought each other no less
furiously, were finally swallowed up in the religion of Jesus.
Out of their ruins, a history, a belief, and a moral and ceremonial code were constructed to which the great mass of
enthusiasts gradually attached themselves.

[All believed in one christ, in a messiah sent by God to
redeem the human race. This was the fundamental dogma
of every sect that wished to raise itself upon the ruins of the
old ones. There were disputes about the time and the place
of his appearance and about his earthly name; but the name
of a prophet who, it was said, had appeared in Palestine,
under Tiberius, eclipsed all others, and the new fanatics
rallied under the standard of the son of Mary.]

As the empire weakened, the faster was the progress of
this Christian religion. The degeneracy of the ancient
conquerors of the world spread to their gods, who, having
presided over their victories, were now merely the impotent
witnesses of their defeats. The spirit of the new sect was
better suited to an age of decadence and misery. Its chief

exponents, for all their impostures and their vices, were enthusiasts ready to perish for their doctrine. The religious zeal of the philosophers and the great men was only a form of political loyalty; and any religion which receives its support merely as a belief useful for the common people to follow, cannot hope for more than a death agony, brief or lengthy. Soon Christianity became a powerful force; it intervened in the quarrels of the Cæsars; it put Constantine on his throne, and then it put itself there beside his feeble successors.

It was in vain that Julian, one of those extraordinary men whom fate sometimes raises to sovereign power, endeavoured to rid the empire of this scourge which was hastening its downfall. His virtues, his indulgent humanity, the simplicity of his ways, the elevation of his mind and character, his talents, his bravery, his military genius and his brilliant victories, all seemed to assure him success. The only reproach that could be levelled against him was that he showed an attachment to a religion become ridiculous that was unworthy of him if he was sincere, and that was ludicrously exaggerated if he was merely politic; but he perished at the height of his glory, after a reign of two years. The colossus of the Roman empire no longer found arms powerful enough to uphold it, and the death of Julian burst the only dam that could still oppose the torrent of the new superstitions and the flood of barbarian invasion.

Disdain for the humane sciences was one of the first characteristics of Christianity. It had to avenge itself against the outrages of philosophy, and it feared that spirit of doubt and inquiry, that confidence in one's own reason which is the bane of all religious beliefs. The natural sciences were odious and suspect, for they are very dangerous to the success of miracles, and there is no religion that does not force its devotees to swallow a few physical absurdities. So the triumph of Christianity was the signal for the complete decadence of philosophy and the sciences.

The sciences might have been able to resist this decadence if the art of printing had been known; as it was, the manu-scripts of any single book were few in number, and to obtain the entire literature of any one science involved considerable difficulty and expense and travelling, which only the rich were able to afford. It was easy for the domi-nant party to effect the disappearance of books that shocked its prejudices or unmasked its impostures. A Barbarian inroad could in one day deprive the whole of a country for ever of the means of education; since the destruction of a single manuscript was often an irreparable loss for a whole country. Besides, only works recommended by the names of their authors were copied. All the research that could acquire importance only if allied to other research, all isolated observations and detailed advances that serve to maintain the sciences at the same level and to prepare a way for further progress, all the materials amassed by time and awaiting genius, remained condemned to eternal obscurity. The converse of scholars and the unification of their labours, which are so useful, at certain times so necessary, did not exist. Each man had to begin and to end a discovery himself, and he was obliged to fight alone against all the obstacles that nature puts in the way of our efforts. Works that facilitate the study of the sciences and illuminate their difficulties, that present truth in simpler and more manageable forms, detailed observations and research that often throw light upon the errors of accepted beliefs, and books in which the reader often grasps what the author himself had not noticed—all these found neither copyists nor readers.

It was thus impossible for the sciences, which already contained such a disordered profusion of knowledge as to make their progress and their further development difficult, to survive, and to resist the slippery slope which led them rapidly to decline. So it is not to be wondered at that Christianity, which after the invention of printing was not powerful enough to prevent their dazzling renaissance, was at this period powerful enough to consummate their ruin.

If we make an exception of dramatic art, which flourished in Athens alone and fell with her, and eloquence, which can only breathe where the air is free, the Greek language and literature long kept its glory. Lucian and Plutarch would not have disfigured the century of Alexander. Rome rose to the level of Greece in poetry, eloquence, history and the art of treating the stark themes of philosophy and the sciences with dignity, elegance and charm. Even Greece never produced a poet who gives such a sense of perfection as Virgil, and she had no historian to equal Tacitus. But this moment of glory was followed by a rapid decline. From the time of Lucian, Rome had none but almost barbarian writers. Chrysostom still spoke the language of Demosthenes; but we cannot recognize the language of Cicero or Livy either in Augustine, or even in Jerome who cannot plead in extenuation the influence of African barbarism.

The truth is that in Rome the study of letters and love of the arts was never a truly popular taste; the transitory perfection of the language was the work, not of the national genius but of certain individuals who had been moulded by the influence of Greece; Roman soil was ever foreign to letters, for though assiduous cultivation could naturalize them, they ran to seed as soon as they were left to themselves.

The importance that was for long ascribed to the talent of the tribune and the bar, in both Greece and Rome, swelled the ranks of the orators in both these countries. Their works have contributed to the progress of that art whose principles and finer points they developed. They also taught another art, however, which has been unduly neglected by the moderns, and which ought to be carried over in our day from spoken works to printed works. This is the art of composing extemporary speeches in which the ordering of the divisions, the method of exposition and

the imagery are all at least tolerable, of addressing an
audience, without any previous preparation and yet without
bewildering them with a string of disordered ideas and a
rambling style, without offending them with extravagant
declamation, uncouth nonsense and fantastic incongruities.
How useful this art would be in all countries where the
functions of position, public office or private interest may
oblige one to speak and to write without having had time
to meditate one's speeches or one's writing! Its history
merits some study, the more so since the moderns, for
whom it is often a necessity, seem to know only of its more
ridiculous aspects.

Throughout this period, books increased in number, and
the interval of time that separated men from the early
Greek writers tended to envelop their writings in obscurity,
so that in consequence the study of books and opinions,
known by the name of erudition, came to occupy an important place in intellectual studies. The library at Alexandria was populated by grammarians and critics. We can
observe in those works of theirs that have come down to us
a tendency to regulate admiration for and confidence in any
book by its age and by the difficulty of understanding it or
of finding it: a disposition to judge opinions not on their
own merits but according to the names of those who held
them: an inclination to trust in authority rather than in
reason; and, finally, the false and pernicious belief in the
decadence of the human race, and the superiority of earlier
ages. The importance that men ascribe to whatever is the
object of their occupations and whatever costs them effort
is at once the explanation of, and the excuse for those errors
in which learned men of all nations and all times have to
some extent participated.

We can reproach the Greek and Roman scholars and
even their scientists and philosophers with a complete lack
of that spirit of doubt which submits facts and proofs to
severe rational scrutiny. As we examine their writings for

an account of events and habits, of natural phenomena, of works of art, we are astonished to see them retail imperturbably the most palpable absurdities, the most revolting extravagances. An *it is said that* or an *it is reported that* at the beginning of a phrase seemed to them sufficient to shelter them from the reproach of puerile credulity. It is, above all, the unfortunate fact that the art of printing was as yet unknown, that accounts for that indifference which corrupted their study of history and opposed their progress in the understanding of nature. The knowledge that one has assembled on every point all the authorities who might confirm or repudiate it, the ability to compare different witnesses, and to understand the controversies to which these differences give rise; all these various ways of ascertaining the truth of some matter cannot exist except when one can have a large number of books and can multiply copies of them indefinitely and is not afraid of their widespread diffusion.

How was there any chance for those travellers' stories and descriptions, of which there was often only a single copy, and which were never submitted to public scrutiny, to acquire that authority which a book can enjoy only when it has been submitted to scrutiny and survived it. In consequence everything was reported equally, because of the difficulty of deciding with any certainty what was worthy of being reported. Nor have we the right to be surprised at the way the most natural and most miraculous facts were presented with precisely the same confidence and precisely the same authority. For in our own day this mistake is still taught in our schools as a principle of philosophy, whilst exaggerated incredulity leads us in the opposite direction to the rejection without examination of everything that seems strange. The science which alone can teach us how to find the point between these two extremes where we should rationally stop is still in its infancy.

THE SIXTH STAGE

The decadence of knowledge to its restoration about the time of the crusades

DURING this disastrous stage we shall witness the rapid decline of the human mind from the heights that it had attained, and we shall see ignorance following in its wake, and sometimes bestial cruelty, and sometimes cruelty in all its refinement, and everywhere corruption and treachery. Nothing could penetrate that profound darkness save a few shafts of talent, a few rays of kindness and magnanimity. Man's only achievements were theological day-dreaming and superstitious imposture, his only morality religious intolerance. In blood and tears, crushed between priestly tyranny and military despotism, Europe awaited the moment when a new enlightenment would allow her to be reborn free, heiress to humanity and virtue.

We must needs divide our picture of this stage into two distinct parts. The first part will deal with the West where decadence ensued more rapidly and more completely, but where the light of reason was to reappear, never again to be extinguished; the second part will deal with the East, where decadence was slower to appear and was for a long time less pervasive, but where even to this day the moment is still awaited when the light of reason will break through and the chains of servitude be cast off.

Christianity had scarcely overthrown the altar of Victory when the West fell a prey to the Barbarians. The conquerors adopted the new religion but not the language of the conquered; this became the preserve of the priests and, thanks to their ignorance and their contempt for letters, whatever might have been hoped for from the study of Latin texts was lost to humanity since they alone could read them.

The ignorance and barbarous morality of the conquerors are well known; yet dull-witted and bestial though they were, it was they who brought about the abolition of domestic slavery, an institution which had besmirched the noblest days of Greece for all her wisdom and her love of liberty. Glebe serfs cultivated the land of the conquerors and provided them with household servants; and this state of affairs flattered their vanity and ensured that their every whim was satisfied. As a result wars were now fought not in order to capture slaves, but so as to acquire land and people to work it. Furthermore most of the slaves whom the conquerors found in the countries that they overran were either members of their own tribes who had been captured in some earlier campaign or else the descendants of such prisoners. A great number of them deserted and joined forces with the armies of the conquerors. Again, the principles of universal brotherhood which were part of the Christian moral code condemned slavery, and the clergy, having in this matter no personal interest in not following maxims which did so much credit to their cause, spoke out openly against slavery, and so served to further its destruction, a consummation which the course of history had now in any case made inevitable.

[This process was the seed of a revolution in the destiny of the human race and to it is due the knowledge of true liberty. It had at first a barely perceptible influence over the fate of the individual. We should have a mistaken idea of slavery in the Ancient World if we compared it to the slavery of the black races of our own day. The Spartans, the nobles of Rome, and the Satraps of the East were in truth barbarous masters. The full cruelty of avarice manifested itself in the work that slaves carried out in the mines. But in most private families masters, out of self-interest, had mitigated the conditions of slavery as far as their household dependents were concerned. In contrast it was comparatively easy to maltreat a glebe serf with impunity, since the law itself granted this at a price. Their degree of dependence was the same as that of the slave, but they received none of the compensations in the matter of care and help. They did not suffer the same continued humiliation, but their masters being vainer were more arrogant. The slave was a man condemned by fate to a condition to which the hazards of war might one day expose his master. The serf was a member of an inferior and degraded class.]

[It is therefore mainly from the point of view of its distant consequences that we ought to consider the destruction of domestic slavery.]

All these barbarian nations had a more or less similar constitution: a common chief called *king*, who with the help of a council pronounced judgments and gave decisions which brooked no delay; an assembly of special chieftains who were consulted on all matters of any importance; and, finally, an assembly of the people where all questions that concerned the people as a whole were deliberated. The principal differences between these three powers lay in the amount of authority they enjoyed; they are to be distinguished not by their functions but by the matters with which they dealt and, even more, by the view of their relative importance held by the mass of the people.

Amongst agricultural peoples and especially amongst those who had already established themselves on foreign territory, these constitutions had acquired a more rigid and determinate character than amongst pastoral peoples. In addition, these nations were dispersed and not brought together in a number of camps. As a result the king had no army constantly at his disposal, and it was not possible for him to follow up his victories by establishing a despotism, which was what generally occurred in Asiatic revolutions.

Thus the conquerors preserved their liberty. They did not destroy the towns although they did not occupy them. Since there was no standing army to maintain a garrison, the towns acquired a measure of independence, and so provided a rallying-place for the spirit of freedom in the conquered nation.

The Barbarians often invaded Italy. They were, however, unable to gain a permanent footing there, because the wealth of the country constantly excited the greed of new invaders, and because the Greeks for a long time clung to the hope of bringing it back within their Empire. As a result, Italy was never totally or permanently reduced to slavery by any nation. The Latin language, which was the sole language of the people, was corrupted more slowly; ignorance was not so complete, nor superstition so crass, as in the other countries of the West.

Rome, which recognized masters only to change them, preserved a species of independence. It was the residence of the head of the church. For whereas in the East the clergy were subject to a single prince, the emperor, whom they sometimes controlled and sometimes conspired against, yet, even when they fought against the despot, they upheld the principle of despotism, preferring to superintend all the power of an absolute monarch rather than possess a limited power for themselves; in the West, on the other hand, the priests, united under a chief of their own, were raised to an eminence of power which rivalled that of the kings, and in divided States constituted a sort of unique and independent monarchy.

[We shall see the overbearing city of Rome attempting to impose the chains of a new tyranny upon the whole world. We shall observe her pontiffs gaining an ascendancy over the ignorant and the credulous by means of crudely forged documents; introducing religion into all the transactions of civil life as the instrument of their avarice or of their vanity; punishing the least opposition to their laws, the least resistance to their absurd prejudices with anathemas terrible to the faithful; maintaining an army of monks in every country, ever ready with their deceits to encourage the superstitious fears, so as to impose fanaticism more effectively; depriving nations of their own forms of worship and of the ceremonies in which their religious hopes were invested so as to plunge them into civil unrest; sowing dissension to obtain power, authorizing treason and perjury, assassination and parricide in the name of God, and making kings and warriors by turn the instruments and the victims of their vengeance; wielding strength but never truly possessing it; terrible to their enemies but trembling before their own defenders; all-powerful at the uttermost ends of Europe yet defied with impunity at the very foot of their own altars; finding in heaven a fulcrum whereby to lever the whole world into motion, but unable to find on earth a regulator for its action; raising a colossus on feet of clay, a colossus which would oppress Europe while it stood and whose ruins were to encumber her long after its fall.]

Wars of conquest had reduced the West to a state of stormy anarchy in which the people groaned under the triple tyranny of kings, warriors and priests; but this anarchy contained the seeds of liberty within its womb.

Our observations about this part of Europe also apply to the countries that were never under Roman rule. Their inhabitants were swept along in the general movement, conquering and conquered by turn; ties of common origin and habits bound them to the conquerors of the Empire and they were indistinguishable from them in most respects. Their political condition observed the same phases and developed in a very similar direction.

We shall trace the picture of the revolutions that mark this stage, which may aptly be called feudal anarchy.

The legislation of the age was savage and uncouth. In so far as we find laws of any mildness, this apparent humanity was really only dangerous indifference. However, there were

at this period a few valuable laws, though these, in so far
as they protected the rights only of the ruling classes were
so much the greater outrage against the universal rights of
mankind; nevertheless, they kept alive a feeble notion of
the rights of man, and were one day to serve as a guide in
their re-discovery and restoration.

[In these laws we find two special customs characteristic
both of the childhood of nations and of the ignorance of
uncivilized ages.]

[A guilty person could buy himself out of punishment by
paying some sum of money fixed by a law which assessed
the value of a man's life by his position or birth. Crimes
were regarded not as attacks against security and the rights
of citizens, something to be prevented by the fear of
punishment, but rather as wrongs done to an individual
which he or his family had the right to avenge but for which
the law offered a more useful reparation. People had so little
idea of the method of proof by which matters of fact could
be established that they found it simpler to ask heaven for
a miracle whenever they wanted to distinguish the guilty
from the innocent, and the outcome of a superstitious trial
by ordeal or the result of a duel were regarded as the surest
methods of discovering and establishing the truth.]

[In a society where independence and liberty were
confused, quarrels even among very minor chieftains de-
generated into private feuds, and these wars between canton
and canton, village and village, were constantly exposing
the whole countryside to all those horrors of war which in
great invasions are at least only temporary, and which in
wars of a more general kind affect only the frontier areas.]

[Whenever tyranny attempts to subject the majority of
the people to the will of a minority, it exploits the prejudices
and ignorance of its victims, and seeks to compensate by
the vigour and unity of a small force for the lack of that
real strength which, it seems, must necessarily belong to
the majority. But the ultimate aim of tyranny, which it only

rarely attains, is to establish real differences between masters and slaves, and so, as it were, to make nature herself an accomplice of political inequality.]

[This was an art actually possessed in ancient times by the priests of the orient, when they were at once kings, pontiffs, judges, astronomers, surveyors, artists and doctors. But what they owed to their monopoly of intelligence, the crude tyrants who ruled over our weak ancestors obtained through institutions and warlike habits. Clad in impenetrable armour, fighting always on horses as invulnerable as themselves, possessing a mastery of horsemanship and arms that could be acquired only after a long and painful apprenticeship, they were able to oppress and kill the common people with impunity; for the people could not afford to buy expensive suits of armour or devote their youth to military exercises, obliged as they were to pursue some useful calling.]

[The tyrannical minority by using this method of fighting acquired a real superiority of strength, which prevented any idea of resistance and for a long time made even acts of desperation useless. And so natural equality disappeared before the artificial inequality of physical force.]

Morality, which was taught by the priests alone, embodied those universal principles upon which all sects have agreed; but it also created a host of purely religious duties and imaginary sins. These duties were more strongly insisted upon than the natural duties; and actions that were neither good nor bad, some that were legitimate and a few that were even virtuous, were more severely reproached and punished than real crimes. However, one moment of repentance, consecrated by a priest's absolution, opened the heavens to a rogue; gifts which flattered the greed of the Church and practices which flattered its vanity sufficed to expiate a whole lifetime of crime. The priests even went so far as to make a tariff for these absolutions. The sins with which they dealt included everything from the most innocent weaknesses of love and the simplest desires to the refinements and excesses of the most vile debauchery. It was obvious that hardly anyone could escape censure, and as a result this was one of the most productive branches of the priestly traffic. They went so far as to assign fixed periods in hell for different offences, which the priests had the power to shorten or even to condone altogether; this indulgence was sold first to the living, and then to the relatives and friends of the dead. They sold acres in heaven for an equivalent number on earth, and were modest enough not to ask for interest.

The morals of these unhappy times were worthy of such a deeply corrupting system.

The growth of this same system gave rise to many absurdities: monks inventing ancient miracles or manufacturing new ones, feeding the ignorance and stupidity of the people with fables and prodigies, deluding them in order to despoil them; doctors of the Church exhausting all their ingenuity in an effort to find some new piece of nonsense with which to embellish their faith or to outdo their predecessors; priests compelling princes to burn any man who dared doubt one of their dogmas, unmask their impostures or denounce their crimes, or who wavered for a moment from the course of blind obedience; so great was their power that they could even send to the stake theologians injudicious enough to dream in a way other than that of their superiors in the Church. . . . Such scenes are all that western Europe has at this stage to contribute to the picture of humanity.

In the East, which was united under a single despot, we shall see decadence pursuing a slower course in the wake of the gradual decay of the empire, and each century's ignorance and corruption becoming greater than those of the preceding one. We see wealth diminish, frontiers contract towards the capital, revolutions become more frequent and tyranny more cowardly and cruel.

As we follow the history of the empire, as we read the books produced by each age, this comparison will strike even the least practised and attentive eye.

In the East people gave themselves even more to theological polemic; it occupied a larger place in history and influenced political events to a greater degree. Daydreams took on subtler forms than the jealous West could as yet achieve, and religious intolerance was as oppressive if less savage.

However the works of Photius show that a taste for rational study was not altogether extinguished. Several emperors and princes and even some princesses did not confine themselves to skill in theological disputation but deigned to cultivate the art of letters.

Roman law changed only gradually as it was corrupted by bad laws which the various emperors passed from greed and love of power or which were wrung from them by the forces of superstition. The Greek language lost its purity and its special character but kept its grammar and verbal wealth; the inhabitants of Constantinople could still read Homer and Sophocles, Thucydides and Plato. Anthemius explained the construction of Archimedes' mirrors, and Proclus used them successfully in the defence of the capital. When the Empire finally fell, Constantinople was still the home of a number of scholars, who fled to Italy where their knowledge proved extremely useful to the progress of enlightenment. During this stage, then, the East had not sunk into the final stage of barbarism, although it was past all hope of mercy. Later it became the prey of the Barbarians; with its disappearance went the last remains of civilization; and the ancient genius of Greece still awaits a liberator.

At the confines of Asia and on the borders of Africa, there existed a people who had been preserved, partly by their bravery, partly by their geographical isolation, from Persian conquests and those of Alexander and the Romans. Of these many tribes, some lived by agriculture whilst others still led a pastoral life. All took part in trade and some in robbery. United by ties of race, language and, to a lesser degree, of religion, they formed one great nation although there was no political link to combine the different parts. Suddenly there arose from amongst them a man of burning enthusiasm and profound astuteness, endowed with the talents of a poet and of a warrior. He conceived the bold design of uniting the Arab tribes into a single community, and was brave enough to execute it. As a first step towards bringing a common rule to a nation which had remained untamed, he founded a more purified religion upon the ruins of the old forms of worship. As legislator, prophet, pontiff, judge, and general, he possessed all the means of subjugating men and knew how to use them skilfully but in the grand manner.

He retailed a number of fables which he claimed to have received from heaven; but he won battles. His life was divided between prayer and the pleasures of love. After twenty years of absolute power, to which there is no precedent in history, he declared that if he had committed a single act of injustice, he was ready to make reparation for it. Everyone was silent; except for one woman alone who had the audacity to claim back a small sum of money. He died, and the enthusiasm that he had communicated to his people was soon to change the face of three-quarters of the world.

The manners of the Arabs were gentle and dignified. They loved poetry and cultivated it; ruling over the most beautiful countries of Asia, they allowed the taste for letters and the sciences to temper their missionary zeal and mitigate their love of war, once time had calmed the fever of religious fanaticism.

They translated Aristotle and studied his works: they cultivated astronomy, optics, and the various branches of medicine; and they enriched these sciences with new truths.

We owe to them the spread of the use of algebra, which had been applied by the Greeks only to one class of problem. If it is true that their fanatical interest in the secrets of alchemy and the elixir of life sullied their work in chemistry, it must be remembered it was they who revived or rather invented this science which had till then been confused with pharmacy or with technical skill in the arts. It was with them that chemistry appeared for the first time as the analysis of bodies into discernible elements and as the theory of their compounds and the laws of such compounds.

With the Arabs the sciences were free, and to this freedom was due their success in reviving some sparks of the Greek genius; but they lived under a despotism sanctified by religion. So this light shone only for a few moments to give way to the blackest darkness; and the work done by the Arabs would have been lost to the human race for ever if they had not done something to prepare the way for the more lasting revival which was brought about in the West.

[So we see for the second time the spirit of genius abandoning a people it had enlightened, and once again it is tyranny and superstition that drove it away. Born in Greece as the twin of liberty, it could neither save it from destruction nor defend reason from the prejudices of men who had already been degraded by slavery. Born amongst Arabs, in the very bosom of despotism and near the cradle of a fanatical religion, it was, like the generous and brilliant character of that people, only a temporary exception to the general laws of nature which condemn servile and superstitious nations to ignorance and degradation.]

[So this second example ought not to cause us anxiety about the future; but it may serve as a warning to the present age to do its utmost to maintain and increase the sum of human knowledge if it wishes to become or to remain free, and to defend that freedom with all its might if it does not wish to lose the advantages that enlightenment has brought it.]

I shall append to the history of the achievement of the Arabs an account of their rapid rise and fall as a nation. After having held sway from the shores of the Atlantic ocean to the banks of the Indus, they lost the greater part of their conquests to the Barbarians, and those countries that they continued to hold served only to exhibit the hideous spectacle of a people degenerate to the last extreme of slavery, corruption and misery. Today they occupy their ancient homeland, maintaining their traditions, their character and their integrity, and have been even able to regain and preserve their ancient independence.

I shall show how the religion of Mahomet, in spite of being of all religions the simplest in dogma, the least absurd in practice and the most tolerant in principle, seems to condemn the whole of that vast area of the earth where its empire has held sway to eternal slavery and incurable stupidity, while at the same time we shall see the genius of science and liberty shining out under the most absurd superstitions and amongst the most barbarous intolerance. China presents the same phenomenon, although there the effects of that stultifying poison have been less grave.

THE SEVENTH STAGE

The early progress of science from its revival in the West to the invention of printing

SEVERAL causes were responsible for the gradual restoration to the human mind of the strength that, it had seemed, would be crushed for ever beneath those heavy, shameful fetters.

The intolerance of the priests, their struggle for political power, their scandalous greed and moral depravity made even more disgusting by a mask of hypocrisy, revolted anyone whose soul was uncorrupted, whose mind unclouded, whose heart undaunted. There was such a striking contrast between the dogmas, principles and behaviour of the priests and those of the early disciples, the founders of their doctrine and moral creed, of whom the priests could scarcely keep the people in total ignorance.

As a result powerful voices were raised against them. In the south of France whole provinces united in adopting a simpler doctrine and a purer form of Christian belief according to which man, subject only to God, might judge according to his own lights what it had pleased God to reveal to him in holy scripture. Armies of fanatics, captained by ambitious leaders, were unleashed upon these provinces. Executioners under the command of priests and legates slaughtered whomsoever the soldiers spared: a tribunal of monks was set up with the task of committing to the executioner anyone who could be suspected of having lent an ear to Reason.

Yet despite such measures, the priests were powerless to prevent this spirit of liberty and free inquiry from spreading surreptitiously. It was repressed in every country where it dared show itself, and wherever intolerant hypocrisy could fan the flames of bloody war; but it managed to survive and secretly spread to another country. It is to be found in all ages up to the moment when, assisted by the invention of *printing*, it was powerful enough to deliver a large area of Europe from the yoke of Rome.

[There already existed a class of men who were above all superstitions and were content to despise them in secret, or at most allowed themselves a few ironical asides in which the mockery was made more telling by the veil of deference with which they were careful to conceal it. The very lightheartedness of these impudent attacks secured their impunity, and appearing, as they did, in works destined only for the amusement of the great or the learned and unread by the ordinary people, they escaped the wrath of any persecutors.]

[Frederick II was suspected of being what our eighteenth-century priests have since called a *philosophe*. The Pope accused him before the whole world of treating the religions of Moses, Jesus and Mahomet as so many politic myths. To his Chancellor, Pietro della Vigna, was attributed a fable called *The Three Impostors*; and although this work was entirely apocryphal, from the title we learn of the existence of an opinion which was the natural consequence of an inquiry into these three beliefs: for springing from a common origin, they must have been corruptions of a purer form of worship rendered by races at the dawn of history to the universal soul of the world.]

[The collections of our own *fabliaux* and the Decameron of Boccaccio are full of passages that breathe this spirit of free inquiry, this scorn for all prejudices and this tendency to make them the subject of a sly and secret derision.]

[This stage thus presents us with the spectacle of men who regarded all superstition with passive contempt side by side with the enthusiastic reformers of its grossest abuses; and we can trace an almost unbroken line of descent for these obscure pronouncements and protestations in favour of the rights of reason going back to the later philosophers of the school of Alexandria.]

[We shall ask ourselves whether, at this period when philosophical proselytism was so formidable, there were not secret societies formed to keep alive a small number of simple truths and to diffuse them clandestinely amongst a few initiates as sure antidotes against the prevalent superstitions.]

[We shall also inquire whether we ought not to number amongst such societies that famous order against which popes and kings conspired so ignobly and which they destroyed so barbarously.]

Priests were obliged to study and perfect themselves in the art of forging biblical passages so as to defend themselves or justify their usurpations of secular power. Kings, for their part, wishing to strengthen their hands in a war in which all claims rested on authority and precedent, encouraged schools for the training of lawyers who could champion them against the priests.

In these disputes between the clergy and governments, and between the clergy of each country and the head of the Church, those endowed with a loftier cast of mind and a franker, nobler character fought on the side of the laity against the priests, on the side of the national clergy against the despotism of a foreign potentate. They attacked these abuses and usurpations and tried to expose their origin. Such boldness may seem to us today mere servile timidity; we are amused to see so much effort spent in proving what ordinary common sense should teach. But these commonplaces were then newly discovered truths, and they often decided the fate of nations; it required independence to pursue them, courage to defend them; and it was through these men that human reason began to recall its rights and its liberty.

In the quarrels that arose between kings and lords, the former gained the support of the large towns by granting them certain privileges or by restoring to them some of their natural human rights; and they sought by manumission to increase the number of those enjoying these civic rights. These men who were reborn to freedom, felt how important it was for them to acquire through the study of law and history that necessary skill and learning which alone could counterbalance the military strength of feudal tyranny.

The rivalry between pope and emperor prevented Italy from being reunited under one master, and ensured the continuance of a large number of independent societies. In small states it is necessary to add the power of persuasion to that of force, and to have recourse to negotiation as often as to arms. As this political warfare had its foundation in a war of ideas, and as Italy had never entirely lost her taste for learning, she became the centre of enlightenment in Europe and, though weak, one that gave promise of rapid growth.

Then, religious enthusiasm fired the western nations to attempt the conquest of the holy places, places consecrated, or so it was said, by the death and miracles of Christ. Not only did this strange distemper assist the progress of liberty by bringing about the impoverishment and decline of the nobility, but it also furthered the relations between Europeans and Arabs, which began with the mingling of Christians and Arabs in Spain and were cemented by the commerce of Pisa, Genoa and Venice. People learnt the Arab language; they read Arab writings; they learnt something about their discoveries, and if in scientific matters they did not go beyond them, at least they had the ambition to rival them.

[These wars, undertaken in the cause of superstition, served to destroy it. The sight of a multiplicity of religions ended by awakening in reasonable men an equal indifference

to creeds which were equally powerless to combat the vices
and the passions of mankind, and an equal scorn for the zeal
equally sincere, equally fanatical with which the different
sects maintained their contradictory doctrines.]

Various republics had been established in Italy, some of
which imitated the forms of the Greek republics whilst
others tried to reconcile the servitude of a subject people
with the democratic liberty and equality of a sovereign
people. In the North, in Germany, some towns had gained
almost complete independence and governed themselves
according to their own laws. In some of the Swiss cantons,
the people broke the chains of feudalism and of the royal
power.

In almost all the great States, mixed constitutions came
into being in which the right to levy taxes and make new
laws was divided sometimes between the king, the nobles,
the clergy and the people, sometimes between the king, the
barons and the commons; in these constitutions the people,
although not yet liberated from their humiliations, at least
had some shelter from oppression, and those who form the
real core of a nation were given the right to defend their
own interests and to be heard in the councils of those who
decided their fate. In England a famous charter was
solemnly sworn by the king and the nobles guaranteeing the
rights of the barons, and some of the rights of ordinary
men.

Other peoples, provinces and even towns obtained similar
charters less well known and less well defended. These are
the originals of those declarations of the rights of man
which all enlightened men to-day regard as the cornerstones
of liberty, but of which the ancients did not and could not
have any notion: since domestic slavery sullied their constitutions, since for them citizenship was a merely hereditary
or adoptive right, and since they were still ignorant of
the inherent rights of the human race which belong to all
men alike.

[In France, in England and in some of the other great nations the people seem to have desired their true rights, but their desire sprang not from enlightened reason but from a blinding sense of oppression, and the only fruit of their efforts was violence avenged by greater violence, looting followed by worse misery.]

[In England, however, the principles of the reformer Wycliffe inspired one of these movements which was led by some of his disciples and which was the precursor of the more elaborate and better organized attempts which the people were to make under other reformers in a more enlightened age.]

The discovery of a manuscript of the code of Justinian occasioned the rebirth of the study of jurisprudence and of legislation and served to mitigate the severity of the law, even amongst the people who knew how to turn it to their advantage without wishing to be restricted by it.

The trade of Pisa, Genoa, Florence and Venice, of the cities of Belgium and some of the free towns of Germany included the Mediterranean and the Baltic and extended to the shores of the European Ocean. Their merchants sought the precious commodities of the Levant in Egyptian ports and on the furthermost shores of the Black Sea.

Politics, legislation and public economy were not as yet sciences; there was no attempt to discover and develop their principles, but experience began to throw some light on these subjects, to supply observations that might form the basis of sciences, and to reveal a state of affairs in which the need for these sciences could not but be felt.

At first the works of Aristotle were known only in translation from the Arabic; and his philosophy, which was at first persecuted, soon reigned supreme in all the schools. It did not make for enlightenment, but it brought greater precision and method to the art of polemic, the child of theological disputes. This scholasticism neither encouraged the discovery of truth nor promoted better methods of evaluating and discussing evidence, but it whetted men's intellects: the taste for subtle distinctions and the need to sharpen ideas to the last refinement, to grasp the most fugitive shades of meaning and to clothe them in new expressions, the whole paraphernalia intended to confound one's opponent or escape his traps—all this was the first beginnings of that philosophical analysis which has since been the fruitful source of our progress.

[We owe to the Schoolmen more precise notions concerning the ideas that can be entertained about the supreme Being and his attributes: the distinction between the first cause and the universe which it is supposed to govern: the distinction between spirit and matter: the different meanings that can be given to the word *liberty*; what is meant by *creation*; the manner of distinguishing the various operations of the human mind, and the correct way of classifying such ideas as it can form of real objects and their properties.]

But this same method could only retard the progress of the natural sciences in the schools. A certain amount of anatomical research, a few obscure works about chemistry entirely taken up with the quest for the Philosopher's Stone, a few works of geometry and algebra which displayed less learning than that possessed by the Arabs and less understanding than that shown by the Ancients, some observations and astronomical calculations which were limited to forming and perfecting tables and which were ludicrously mixed up with astrology; such is the picture of the sciences of this age. However the mechanical arts began to approach the perfection that they had attained in Asia. Silk production was introduced into the countries of southern Europe and windmills and paper mills were built. The art of measuring time progressed beyond the point to which the Ancients and the Arabs had brought it. Finally, two important discoveries mark this stage of history. The property which the magnet possesses of always turning towards the same point in the sky, which the Chinese knew

of and used for sailing, was also discovered in Europe. Men
learnt the use of the compass and so trade increased, the art
of navigation was perfected and men's thoughts turned to
those voyages of discovery which have opened up a new
world and allowed man to survey the whole expanse of the
globe on which he has been set. A chemist, mixing saltpetre
with inflammable matter, found the secret of that power
which produced an unexpected revolution in the art of war.
Despite the terrible effects of firearms, by allowing com-
batants to fight at a greater distance from one another, they
have made war less murderous and warriors less ferocious.
Military expeditions are now more costly; wealth can
balance strength and even the most bellicose nations need
to make themselves rich through the cultivation of trade
and the arts if they are ever to possess the means of making
war. Organized countries no longer have to fear the blind
courage of barbarous nations. Vast conquests and the
revolutions that follow in their wake have become almost
impossible. The superiority that the wearing of armour,
the possession of horses that were almost invulnerable, and
the use of the lance, the sword and the club gave the nobility
over the common people disappeared, and the destruction
of this last obstacle to freedom and to real equality is due
to an invention which seemed at first glance to threaten the
human race.

In Italy the language had almost reached perfection by
the fourteenth century. Dante can be noble, precise and
vigorous. Boccaccio's language has grace, simplicity and
elegance. The ingenious and sensitive Petrarch has not aged.
In this country with a climate so agreeably similar to that
of Greece, the masters of antiquity were studied and people
tried to carry across into the new language some of their
beauties or to imitate them in the old. Some of their efforts
already held out the hope that, awakened by the sight of
these monuments of antiquity, instructed by these dumb
but eloquent examples, the genius of the arts was about to

embellish man's existence for the second time, and to offer
him those pure pleasures whose enjoyment is open to all
and which increases as it is shared.

The rest of Europe followed far behind; but the taste for
letters and poetry at least began to refine languages that
were still barbarous.

The causes that had forced men to emerge from their
long lethargy, also influenced the direction that their activity took. Reason was never called upon to decide those
matters where there was any real conflict of interests; religion, far from recognizing the authority of reason, claimed
to overrule it and glorified in its humiliation; and politics,
in deciding what was just, always respected whatever was
consecrated by habit, ancient customs, and convention.

It was not suspected that the rights of man were written
in the book of nature and that to look for them in any other
was to misunderstand and outrage them. It was rather to
holy books, revered authors, Papal bulls, royal edicts,
cartularies of custom and church chronicles that people
turned for rules and precedents by which they could guide
their conduct. There was no question of examining a
principle in its own right: it was always a matter of interpreting, discussing, attacking, supporting one set of quota-
tions by appeal to another. A proposition was accepted not
because it was true, but because it was written in such-and-
such a book and had been recognized in such-and-such a
country since such-and-such a date.

In this way the authority of men was everywhere substituted for the authority of reason. Books were studied
much more than nature, and the opinions of the ancients
instead of the phenomena of the universe. This slavery of
the mind from which there was as yet no chance of appeal
to an enlightened criticism, was more harmful to the
progress of human kind by reason of its corrupting influences on all study than in any of its immediate consequences. Men were so far short of the standard of the

ancients that the time had not come to try to correct or surpass them.

Throughout this stage manners preserved their corruption and ferocity; religious intolerance was more active than ever; and civil discords, the endless wars of a crowd of petty princes, replaced the invasions of the Barbarians and the more sinister scourge of private warfare. It is true that the gallantry of minstrels and troubadours and the institution of chivalry which encouraged liberality and sincerity and was devoted to the maintenance of religion, the defence of the oppressed and the service of the ladies, seem to have imparted some gentleness, refinement and elevation to manners. But this change was confined to the courts and castles and did not reach the mass of the people. It brought about a little more equality between the nobles, less treachery and cruelty in their relations with one another; but their contempt for the people, the violence of their tyranny, the audacity of their brigandage remained the same; and the nations, as oppressed as ever, lay as ever in a state of ignorance, barbarism and corruption.

The poetry, the gallantry and the martial qualities of chivalry, due in large part to the Arabs whose natural generosity long resisted superstition and despotism in Spain, were doubtless useful; they sowed the seeds of humanity which were to bear fruit only in more fortunate times; and it was indeed, the general character of this stage that it disposed the human mind for the revolution that the discovery of printing must bring about, and that it prepared the soil on which future generations were to produce so rich and abundant a harvest.

THE EIGHTH STAGE

From the invention of printing to the time when philosophy and the sciences shook off the yoke of authority

To those who have not reflected much upon the progress of the human spirit in the sphere of scientific discovery or of artistic method, it might well seem amazing that such a long period of time should have elapsed between the discovery of the art of printing designs and the discovery of the art of printing characters. Doubtless some engravers had thought of such an application of their art; but the difficulties of its execution had weighed with them more than the benefits of success; and it is indeed fortunate that nobody had suspected the full extent of future success, for priests and kings would surely have united to smother at birth an enemy who was to unmask and dethrone them.

With printing the copies of any book can be multiplied indefinitely at little cost. Since its invention, it has been possible for anyone who could read to obtain any book that he wanted or needed; and this which made reading easier in turn increased the will to learn and the means of instruction.

With so many copies of a book in circulation at the same time, information about facts and discoveries reached a wider public, and also reached it more promptly. Knowledge became the subject of a brisk and universal trade.

Previously people had had to search for manuscripts just as today we search for rare books. What formerly only a few individuals had been able to read, could now be read by a whole nation and could reach almost at the same moment everyone who understood the same language.

Men found themselves possessed of the means of communicating with people all over the world. A new sort of tribunal had come into existence in which less lively but deeper impressions were communicated; which no longer allowed the same tyrannical empire to be exercised over men's passions but ensured a more certain and more durable power over their minds; a situation in which the advantages are all on the side of truth, since what the art of communication loses in the power to seduce, it gains in the power to enlighten. The public opinion that was formed in this way was powerful by virtue of its size, and effective because the forces that created it operated with equal strength on all men at the same time, no matter what distances separated them. In a word, we have now a tribunal, independent of all human coercion, which favours reason and justice, a tribunal whose scrutiny it is difficult to elude, and whose verdict it is impossible to evade.

New methods, accounts of the first stages on the road to some discovery, the work that makes it possible, the ideas that suggest it or inspire men to it, all these become readily available as a result of printing, and offer to every man the whole store of methods and techniques that has been produced by the efforts of others; and it is as a consequence of this mutual assistance that genius has been able to more than double its strength.

Any new mistake is criticized as soon as it is made, and often attacked even before it has been propagated; and so it has no time to take root in men's minds. Those fallacies which are imbibed in infancy, becoming in some way identified with the reason of the individual, and which weaker characters cling to out of terror or hope, have now been eradicated for this reason alone—that it has become impossible to prevent their being openly discussed, to disguise the fact that they can be attacked and rejected, or to maintain them against the progress of truth which by argument must ultimately reveal them as absurd.

It is to printing that we are indebted for the fact that it is now possible to circulate any book required by the circumstances of the moment or the transitory changes of opinion, and, in consequence, all men who speak the same language can become alive to any question discussed anywhere.

Without this art, how would it be possible to produce in adequate numbers books suited to the different classes of men and to the different degrees of education? Prolonged discussion which alone can cast an unwavering light on doubtful questions and establish on an unshakable foundation truths that are too abstract, too subtle, too far-removed from the prejudices of the vulgar or the accepted opinion of the learned not to be soon forgotten and misunderstood; elementary books, dictionaries, works of reference containing a host of facts, observations and experiments in which all proofs are developed and all doubts discussed; valuable compilations containing all that has been observed, written or thought about one particular branch of the sciences, or setting out the work of all the scientists of one country in a given year; tables and diagrams of all kinds, some that show us conclusions that our minds would otherwise have grasped only after long struggle, some to which we can refer for some fact, observation, sum, formula, or object that we need, and others that give us in a convenient form, in a methodical arrangement, the materials from which genius can extract new truths: all these means of accelerating, assisting, ensuring the forward march of the human mind must be numbered amongst the blessings brought by printing.

We shall reveal still more of these benefits when we come to analyse the effects of abandoning, in the sciences, a language common to the scholars of all countries, in favour of the vernacular.

Has not printing freed the education of the people from all political and religious shackles? It would be vain for any despotism to invade all the schools; vain for it to issue cruel edicts prescribing and dictating the errors with which men's minds were to be infected, and the truths from which they were to be safeguarded; vain for the chairs dedicated to the moral enlightenment of the vulgar or the instruction of the young in philosophy and the sciences to be obliged under duress to put forward nothing but opinions favourable to the maintenance of this double tyranny: printing would still be able to diffuse a clear and independent light. The instruction that every man is free to receive from books in silence and solitude can never be completely corrupted. It is enough for there to exist one corner of free earth from which the press can scatter its leaves. How with the multitude of different books, with the innumerable copies of each book, of reprints that can be made available at a moment's notice, how could it be possible to bolt every door, to seal every crevice through which truth aspires to enter? For though this was difficult enough even when it was only a question of destroying a few copies of a manuscript to annihilate it for ever, of proscribing a book or an opinion for a few years to consign it to eternal oblivion, has it not become impossible today when it would be necessary to maintain an absolutely ceaseless vigilance and an unresting activity? For even if it were possible to suppress those truths which only too obviously and directly injure the interests of the inquisitors, how would it be possible to suppress those other truths which secretly or by implication contain the forbidden truths within them, and which one day would lead mankind back to them? Could it be done at all without dropping the mask of hypocrisy, and would not this be almost as fatal as truth itself to the power of error? So we shall see reason triumphing over all such vain attempts, and we shall see it, in this ever recurrent and often cruel war, overcoming violence as well as cunning, braving the executioners and resisting the tempters, crushing under its all-powerful hand, first, religious hypocrisy which demands sincere adoration for its dogmas and, then, the political hypocrisy which abjectly pleads that it may be allowed to profit in peace from those errors in which, if we are to believe it, it is profitable not only for itself but for mankind that mankind should be sunk for ever.

There are two other events which took place almost at the same time as the invention of printing, of which one exerted an immediate influence over the progress of the human mind whereas the influence of the other will be felt as long as the human race endures. I speak of the capture of Constantinople by the Turks, and the discovery of the New World and of the route that opened direct communication between Europe and the eastern parts of Africa and Asia.

The Greek men of letters, fleeing from the domination of the Tartars, sought refuge in Italy. They taught people to read the poets, orators, historians, philosophers and scientists of ancient Greece in the original language; they increased first of all the number of manuscripts and then the number of editions. People were no longer confined to the worship of what had officially passed for the doctrine of Aristotle, but now looked to his own writings for what t had really been; they had the courage to criticize it and attack it, and Plato was set up in opposition. Once people felt that they had the right to choose their master, they had already begun to throw off the yoke.

The reading of Euclid, Archimedes, Diophantus, Hippocrates, Aristotle's History of Animals and even his Physics revived the genius of geometry and physics, and the anti-Christian opinions of the philosophers fanned the all but extinguished notions of the ancient rights of human reason.

Intrepid men, inspired by love of glory and passion for discovery, had pushed back further the bounds of the universe for Europe, had shown her new skies and opened

up unknown lands. Da Gama had reached India after
following the long African coastline with unwearying
patience, whilst Columbus, abandoning himself to the
waves of the Atlantic Ocean, had discovered that hitherto
unknown world which lies to the west of Europe and to the
east of Asia.

If this passion, whose restless activity henceforth
embraced all objects, presaged great progress for the human
race, if noble curiosity animated the heroes of navigation,
it was a base, pitiless greed, a stupid, fierce fanaticism that
inspired the kings and ruffians who were to profit from
their labours. The unfortunate creatures who lived in these
new lands were treated as though they were not human
beings because they were not Christians. This prejudice,
which had an even more degrading effect on the tyrants
than on their victims, smothered any feeling of remorse
that might have touched these greedy and barbarous men,
spewed up from the depths of Europe, and they abandoned
themselves to their insatiable thirst for blood and gold. The
bones of five million men covered those unfortunate lands
where the Portuguese and the Spaniards brought their
greed, their superstitions and their wrath. They will lie
there to the end of time as a mute witness against the
doctrine of the political utility of religion; a doctrine which
even to this day finds its apologists amongst us.

For the first time man knew the globe that he inhabited,
was able to study in all countries the human race as modified
by the long influence of natural causes or social institutions,
and could observe the products of the earth or of the sea,
in all temperatures and all climates. The wealth of every
kind which these natural resources offer to men, and which
is so far from being exhausted that its vast extent is as yet
not even suspected; a knowledge of the natural world that
can furnish new truths and destroy accredited errors in the
sciences; the increased activity of trade which has given new
wings to industry and navigation and, by a necessary chain

of influence, to all the sciences and to all the arts; and the
strength which this activity has given to free nations to
resist tyrants, to enslaved people to break their chains or at
least to relax the chains of feudalism: all these are also to be
numbered amongst the fortunate consequences of these
discoveries. But these discoveries will have repaid humanity
what they have cost it only when Europe renounces her
oppressive and avaricious system of monopoly; only when
she remembers that men of all races are equally brothers
by the wish of nature and have not been created to feed the
vanity and greed of a few privileged nations; only when she
calls upon all people to share her independence, freedom
and knowledge, which she will do once she is alive to her
own true interests. Unfortunately we must still ask ourselves
if this revolution will be the honourable fruit of the progress
of philosophy or only, as it has hitherto been, the shameful
consequence of national jealousies and the excesses of
tyranny.

Up to this stage, the crimes of the clergy had gone
unpunished. The protestations of oppressed humanity and
of outraged reason had been smothered in blood and flames.
But the spirit that had inspired these protests was not
extinguished, though a terrified silence encouraged men to
carry out further monstrous deeds. At last the scandalous
practice of farming out the absolution of sins to monks and
their selling it in taverns and public places caused a new
explosion. Luther, holding in one hand the holy books,
pointed out with the other how the Pope had arrogated to
himself the right of absolving crimes and selling pardons;
how he exercised an insolent despotism over bishops who
were his equals; how the brotherly breaking of bread of the
first Christians had become, under the name of the *mass*, a
sort of magic operation and an object of trade; how the
priests were condemned to the corruption of irrevocable
celibacy; how a barbarous and scandalous law pertained to
monks and nuns whose pontifical ambition had flooded

the Church and sullied her; how through confession the secrets of laymen were delivered up to the plots and passions of the priests; finally, how God himself played only a small part in the prayers that were lavished on bread, men, bones or statues.

Luther announced to the astonished masses that these revolting institutions were not Christianity, but were its depravity and shame, and that, to be faithful to the religion of Jesus Christ, one must first abjure the religion of the priests. He used in equal measure the weapons of dialectic and learning and the no less powerful ones of ridicule. He wrote both in German and in Latin. The situation was very different from what it had been in the days of the Albigensians or of John Hus whose doctrines, unknown outside their own churches, could be so easily calumnied: for the German books of the new apostles reached all the important villages of the Empire while their Latin writings aroused the whole of Europe from the shameful slumber into which superstition had plunged her. Those whose reason had anticipated the reformers in their suggestions but who had been frightened into silence, those who were disturbed by grave doubts, though too terrified to admit them even to themselves, those simpler men who had not realized the full extent of the absurdities of theology, and those who having never reflected on these contested questions were astonished to learn that they must choose between conflicting opinions: all these gave themselves over eagerly to these discussions on which they saw that both their earthly interests and their future felicity depended.

All Christian Europe, from Sweden to Italy, from Hungary to Spain was overrun by the upholders of the new doctrines, and reform would have delivered all the inhabitants of Europe from the yoke of Rome, had not the misguided politics of a few princes supported the very sacerdotal sceptre which had so often been laid on the heads of kings.

Their policy, which unfortunately their successors have not yet abjured, was to ruin their own states in order to acquire new ones, and to measure their power by the extent of their territories rather than by the number of their subjects.

Thus Charles V and Francis I, who were engaged in a struggle for Italy, sacrificed the profit to be derived from reform to their own interest in remaining friendly with the Pope.

The Emperor, seeing that the princes of the Empire favoured opinions which would add to their power and wealth, made himself the protector of the old religion in the hope that a religious war would give him an opportunity to invade their states and to destroy their independence. Francis imagined that, by burning Protestants in his own country and protecting their leaders in Germany, he could keep the Pope's good will without losing valuable allies.

But this was not the only motive at work. Despotism also has its instincts, and these instincts had taught kings that, once religious prejudice had been subjected to the examination of reason, men would soon submit political prejudices to the same examination; that when they were enlightened about Papal usurpations they would then want enlightenment about royal usurpations; and that the reform of ecclesiastical abuses which was so useful to royal power would carry in its wake that of the more oppressive abuses on which that power itself was founded. Thus no king of a great nation voluntarily took the side of the reformers. Henry VIII, on whom papal anathema had been pronounced, continued to persecute them; Edward and Elizabeth, who could not attach themselves to Papism without declaring themselves usurpers, founded in England a system of belief and manner of worship that was as close to it as possible. The Protestant monarchs of Great Britain have invariably favoured Catholicism whenever it has not threatened them with a pretender to their throne.

In Sweden and Denmark the establishment of Lutheranism was only a necessary precaution in royal eyes to make sure of the expulsion of the Catholic tyrant whom the kings themselves replaced. We see too in the Prussian monarchy which was founded by a philosophical prince, that his successor could not hide a secret leaning towards this religion so dear to kings.

Religious intolerance was common to all sects, and they inspired all governments with it. The Papists persecuted all the reformed sects; and these in turn, though full of mutual hatreds, united against the anti-Trinitarians, who in a more rational frame of mind had subjected all dogmas equally, if not to the examination of reason, at least to some form of rational criticism and had not thought they could only free themselves from some absurdities in order to keep others just as revolting.

This intolerance played into the hands of the Papists. There had long existed in Europe and especially in Italy a class of men who rejected all superstitions, were indifferent to all forms of worship, acknowledged only the supremacy of reason, and regarded all religions as the invention of man; but though they might ridicule religion in private, prudence and practical policy demanded that they paid it all the outward marks of respect. Later, boldness was carried further: and whilst in the schools the misunderstood Aristotelian philosophy was used to perfect the art of theological casuistry and to give an air of subtlety to what would otherwise have appeared absurd, some scholars attempted to found, on the basis of his genuine doctrine, a system destructive of all religious ideas, a system in which the human soul was regarded as merely a faculty which faded away when life came to an end and in which no other guide or commander of the world was admitted but the necessary laws of nature. They were opposed by the Platonists whose own views, approximating to what has since been called deism, were even more terrifying from the point of view of priestly orthodoxy.

The fear of punishment and torture soon put an end to

such imprudent frankness. Italy and France were sullied with the blood of martyrs for the freedom of thought. All sects and governments and every authoritarian body were in accord on this alone: that they were against reason. Reason had to be covered with a veil which hid it from the gaze of tyrants but let it be seen by philosophy.

So it became necessary to retire once more into the timid reserve of that secret doctrine which had never been without a considerable body of adherents. It was widespread among the heads of State and Church; and, about the time of the Reformation, the principles of religious Machiavellianism had become the only belief of princes, ministers and pontiffs. Such opinions had even corrupted philosophy. For what morality could really be expected from a system one of whose principles was that the morality of the people must be founded on false opinions, that enlightened men are right to deceive others provided that they supply them with useful errors, and that they may justifiably keep them in the chains that they themselves have known how to break? If the natural equality of men, the cornerstone of their rights, is the basis of all true morality, what can be hoped for from a philosophy one of whose maxims is an open scorn for this equality and these rights? Doubtless this same philosophy made some contribution to the progress of reason, whose reign it prepared in silence, but, as long as it existed alone, it did nothing but substitute hypocrisy for fanaticism and corrupt those who presided over the destinies of states, even when it raised them above prejudice.

The truly enlightened philosophers, strangers to ambition, who allowed themselves to deceive men only with the utmost reluctance and had no wish to see them kept in their errors, would in the natural course of events have embraced the cause of Reform, but, rebuffed by finding the same intolerance everywhere, most of them could see no reason why they should expose themselves to the embarrassments of conversion if after this conversion they would be no freer than they had been before. As long as there was any need to simulate a belief in absurdities which they rejected, they saw little advantage in diminishing in some small degree the number of these absurdities; they even feared that they would give themselves the look of voluntary hypocrisy by this recantation: and so, by remaining attached to the old religion, they strengthened it with the authority of their names.

The spirit that animated the reformers did not lead to true freedom of thought. Each religion allowed, in the country where it dominated, certain opinions only. However, as these diverse beliefs were opposed to each other, there were few opinions that were not attacked or upheld in some part of Europe. Besides, the new religious assemblies had been forced to relax somewhat their dogmatic strictness. They could not without crudely contradicting themselves limit too narrowly the right of free inquiry since it was by appeal to this very same right that they had justified their own separation from the established religion. Even if they refused to give reason its full freedom, they yet allowed its prison to be less narrow: the chain was not broken but it was less heavy and less constricting. Finally, in those countries where it had been impossible for one religion to oust all others, there was established what the dominant cult in its boldness dared to name tolerance, that is, a licence given by men to other men to believe what their reason inclines them to believe, to do what their conscience orders them to do, and to give to their common God the homage that they believe will please him best. One could then profess any tolerated doctrine with a more or less complete frankness.

In this way there arose in Europe a sort of freedom of thought, not for all men, but for all Christians; and indeed if we except France, it is only Christians who enjoy this freedom everywhere today.

But intolerance forced human reason to inquire into those

rights which had been too long forgotten, or, rather, which
had never been well known or properly explained.

Some generous-hearted men indignant at seeing people
oppressed, even in the sanctuary of their conscience, by
kings who were either superstitious slaves or the political
instruments of the priesthood, dared at last to examine the
basis of this priestly power, and they demonstrated to the
people this great truth: that liberty is an inalienable good,
that tyranny has no prescriptive right, that no convention
can tie a nation irrevocably to a single family, that the
magistrates, whatever their rights, functions and powers
may be, are the servants of the people and not its masters,
that the people retain the power to take away authority
from them, if it is abused or even if the people think that
it is no longer in their interests to leave it where it is, for this
authority emanates from the people, and, finally, that the
people have the right to punish their magistrates as well as
the right to revoke their powers.

Such were the opinions that Althusius and Languet and
later Needham and Harrington bravely professed and
forcefully expounded. In conformity with the spirit of
their times, however, they relied too much and too often
on texts, authorities and predecents, and it is obvious that
they owed their opinions much more to the elevation of
their minds and their strength of character than to any exact
analysis of the true principles of the social order.

However, other more timid philosophers were content to
insist on an exact parity of rights and duties between people
and kings and a mutual obligation to keep their agreement.
It was quite possible to depose and punish a hereditary
magistrate but only if he had violated the sacred contract,
and the contract itself continued to hold good between the
people and his descendants. This doctrine, which swept
aside natural right and referred all matters back to positive
law, was supported by jurists and theologians; it was a view
that was in harmony with the interests of the powerful and

the designs of the ambitious: for it was less a stricture upon power itself than upon those who exercised it. And so it was almost invariably adopted by publicists, and it came to be employed as the theoretical basis of all revolutions and political dissension.

[History shows us at this period little real progress towards liberty but greater strength and order in governments, and among the people a livelier and juster sense of their rights. Laws are better formulated and appear less often to be the vague product of circumstance and caprice; they are made by learned men if not yet by philosophers.]

The popular movements and revolutions that had convulsed the states of Italy, England and France were destined to draw the attention of philosophers to that part of politics which consists in observing and predicting the effects of different constitutions, laws and public institutions upon the freedom and prosperity of the people as well as upon the power of states, the preservation of their independence and the form of their governments. Some philosophers like More and Hobbes imitated Plato, in deducing from certain general principles a plan for a whole system of social order and in constructing a model to which all practice was supposed to conform. Others, like Machiavelli, tried to find, after a profound scrutiny of the facts of history, general rules by means of which they could give themselves the illusion of mastering the future.

[Economic science did not yet exist. Princes counted not the number of men but the number of soldiers, and finance was only the art of robbing people without goading them into revolt. Governments interested themselves in commerce only in order to enfeeble it by taxation, restrict it through privileges, or dispute its monopoly amongst themselves.]

The nations of Europe, busy with the interests which genuinely united them and with those which they imagined divided them, felt the need for the recognition of certain rules between themselves which, even independently of treaties, would control their peaceful relations with each other, and for the invention of others which would be respected in times of war so as to soften its ferocity, diminish its ravages and prevent unnecessary hardship. There existed a science of the law of nations, but unfortunately this law was drawn not from reason and nature, the only authorities that ought to be acknowledged by free nations, but from established customs and the beliefs of antiquity. In all this human rights and justice towards individuals were consulted less than the ambition, the greed and the vanity of governments.

We do not find moralists at this time inquiring into the human heart or analysing man's faculties and sentiments with the aim of discovering the nature, origin, rule and sanction of his duties. On the contrary, we see them using all the subtlety of scholasticism to discover in the case of actions whose morality is in doubt the precise point where innocence ends and sin begins; to determine what authority carries the necessary weight to justify in practice one of these doubtful actions; to enumerate methodically the various sins according to their type and gravity; and, above all, to distinguish those which merit eternal damnation.

It was impossible for there to be any science of morality, since the priests enjoyed the exclusive privilege of interpreting and judging actions. But these very subtleties, ridiculous and scandalous though they were, helped to discover and to assess the morality and motives of different actions; the order and limit of duties; and the principles according to which a choice was to be made if these duties conflict: much as the study of a crude machine may help a clever mechanic to build a new and less imperfect one.

[The Reformation by abolishing confession, indulgences, monastic life and priestly celibacy purified the principles of morality, and elevated manners in those countries which embraced it. It delivered them from the expiation of sins

I

by priests, a dangerous encouragement to crime, and from religious celibacy which, being itself the enemy of the domestic virtues, is the destroyer of all virtues.]

This stage in our history was more than any other besmirched by terrible atrocities. It was the time of the religious massacres, the holy wars and the depopulation of the New World.

[It saw the re-establishment of the old slavery in forms more barbarous than ever and more fecund in unnatural crime; it saw the avarice of traders who trafficked in human life, selling men as merchandise having bought them by treachery, piracy or murder, carrying them to one hemisphere where they could live for the sake of the inhabitants of the other, under circumstances of humiliation and outrage and slow, prolonged suffering.]

At the same time hypocrisy filled Europe with butchers and murderers. The monster of fanaticism, angered by its wounds, seemed to redouble its ferocity and to pile up its victims the faster that reason threatened to wrest them from its grip. We can see, however, some of the gentle, courageous virtues reappear to honour and console humanity. History offers us names that can be pronounced without blushing; strong, pure souls, and men of noble character allied to great talent stand out against these scenes of treachery, corruption and carnage. The human race still revolts the philosopher who contemplates its history; but it no longer humiliates him, and now offers him hope for the future.

The progress of the sciences was swift and startling. The language of algebra was generalized, simplified and perfected, or rather it was only at this period that it was at all rigorously formed. The first foundations of the general theory of equations were laid down, the nature of the solutions that it gave was investigated, and equations of the third and fourth degree were solved.

The ingenious invention of logarithms which abridge arithmetical operations and facilitate all the applications of mathematics to real objects, extended the sphere of all those sciences in which applications to particular cases are one of the means of comparing a hypothesis or a theory with the facts and so of arriving at the discovery of natural laws. In mathematics indeed the length and purely practical complications of calculation set a limit beyond which time and energy cannot advance; a term which without the help of these ingenious abbreviations would mark the limits of the science itself, and the frontier which all the efforts of genius could not transcend.

The law of falling bodies was discovered by Galileo, who deduced from it the theory of uniform acceleration and calculated the curve described by a body thrown into space at a determinate speed and moved by a force constantly acting upon it in parallel directions.

Copernicus revived the correct theory of the system of the universe which had been forgotten for so long and eradicated it from anything that was repellent to sensory experience by means of the theory of apparent movements. He set up the extreme simplicity of real movements that results from this system in contrast to the almost fatuous complexity of those demanded by the Ptolemaic hypothesis. The movements of the planets were determined with greater accuracy, and Kepler's genius discovered the form of their orbits and the constant laws that regulate them.

Galileo applied the recent discovery of the telescope perfected by himself to astronomy, and in this way revealed new heavens to the eyes of man. The spots that he observed on the surface of the sun enabled him to discover the fact of its rotation and he determined the time and the laws of this. He demonstrated the phases of Venus and discovered the four moons that surround Jupiter and accompany it in its vast orbit. He learnt how to measure time exactly by means of the oscillations of a pendulum.

So man owes to Galileo the first mathematical theory of motion that was not at once uniform and rectilinear, and the first knowledge of one of the mechanical laws of nature; he owes the discovery of another of these empirical laws to Kepler, a discovery which is doubly advantageous since it leads to the knowledge of the mechanical law whose result they explain, and supplements this knowledge with what would otherwise never have been attained by man.

The discovery of the weight of air and the circulation of the blood mark the progress of experimental physics, which was born in the school of Galileo, and of anatomy, which was already so advanced as to have become separated from pharmacy.

Natural history, chemistry, despite its fantastic hopes and its puzzling language, medicine and surgery astonish us by the speed of their progress, though they often offend us by the spectacle of the monstrous prejudices that still adhere to them.

[Passing over the works of Gesner and Agricola in which there is a great deal of genuine science mixed with a certain amount of error derived both from learned and from vulgar sources, we come to Bernard de Palissy who taught mankind how the quarries from which it hews the materials for its buildings and the rock formations that it knows as mountains, are made up out of the bodies of sea-animals and are thus monuments to the ancient cataclysms that convulsed the globe; and he explained how water is sucked up from the sea by evaporation, is given back to it in the form of rain, and then either soaks through the earth until it reaches the layers of clay or forms glaciers upon the mountains and so sustains the eternal flow of fountains, rivers and seas. Meanwhile Jean Rey discovered the secret of those combinations of air with metallic substances, the first seed of the brilliant theories that have recently extended the bounds of chemistry.]

In Italy the art of epic poetry, painting and sculpture attained a degree of perfection unknown to the Ancients. In the works of Corneille we see that dramatic art in France was close to attaining even greater heights; indeed, if an enthusiasm for antiquity claims a certain superiority of genius for the men who created its masterpieces, it is very difficult for anyone who compares their works with the productions of Italy and France not to perceive the real progress that the art itself has made at the hands of the moderns.

By this time, the Italian language was fully formed, and every day those of other nations lost some vestige of ancient barbarousness.

The influence of metaphysics and grammar was beginning to be felt, and analysis and philosophical explanation were applied more extensively to the rules and common usage governing the formation of words and phrases.

Everywhere during this stage we see reason and authority fighting for supremacy, a battle which prepared and anticipated the triumph of reason.

It is then that the critical spirit was born which alone can make learning really useful. Men still felt the need to know everything that the Ancients had done; but they began to understand that if they were obliged to admire them, they were also permitted to judge them. Reason, which sometimes leant on authority and was more often opposed by it, wished to know what she could expect from it in the way of assistance and what grounds there could be for making the sacrifices that it demanded of her. Those who took authority as the foundation of opinion and the guide to conduct felt how imperative it was for them to make certain of the real strength of their position, so as to avoid the danger of being overwhelmed at the first onslaught of reason.

The practice of writing exclusively in Latin on scientific, philosophical, legal, even historical subjects was, in each country, gradually replaced by the use of the vernacular. This is the moment to examine the influence of this change on the progress of the human mind, for it made the sciences more popular at the price of making it more difficult for scientists to follow their general progress; it allowed the less educated people of a country to read a book written in that country, but it stood in the way of its being read by the enlightened of all Europe; it relieved a large number of men, thirsty for knowledge, without either the time or the means to acquire an extensive and deep erudition, from the necessity of learning Latin; but it forced the learned to spend more time in the study of several different languages.

We shall show that, once it had become impossible to make Latin a popular language common to all Europe, the continued use of it in the literature of the sciences could have had only a transitory usefulness; that the existence of a sort of scientific language, the same for all nations, alongside the different languages spoken by the ordinary people of each country, would have divided men into two classes, perpetuated prejudice and error, and placed an irremovable obstacle in the way of true equality in the use of reason and in the acquisition of necessary truths; and that, if the progress of the masses of the human race had in this way been suspended, ultimately, as in the East, the progress of the sciences themselves would have come to a stop.

For a long time education had been confined to the church and the cloister.

The universities were still dominated by priests. Although they had had to surrender part of their influence to the government, they still retained complete authority over primary and general education, and over the education necessary for all the ordinary professions, for all classes of men, and so exercised control during the years of childhood and youth when the flexible intelligence and uncertain, pliant soul can be shaped at will. All that they conceded to the secular power was the right to direct the study of jurisprudence and medicine, higher education in the sciences, literature and the classical languages; these secular schools were few in number, and only men were sent there who had already been bent under the priestly yoke.

The clergy lost this influence in those countries which had embraced the Reformed religion. In these countries, popular education, though dependent on the government, did not cease to be guided by the theological spirit; but it was not exclusively in the hands of the members of the presbytery. It continued to corrupt men's minds with religious prejudices; but it did not bend them any longer under the yoke of priestly authority. It still produced fanatics, visionaries, and sophists; but it no longer produced slaves to superstition.

Teaching, however, was everywhere in a state of bondage and everywhere exercised a corrupting influence, crippling the minds of children with the weight of religious prejudices and stifling the spirit of liberty in older students with political prejudices.

Not only did anyone who tried to educate himself find the solid and fearful phalanx of all the errors of his country and his century standing between himself and the truth but the most dangerous of these errors were, so to speak, already part of himself. Every man had to begin by recognizing his own errors before he could dispel those of others, and before wrestling with the natural difficulties placed in the way of truth he had as it were to refashion his own intelligence. Education had given him some instruction but before it could be made to serve any useful purpose, it had to be purged and purified of the mists in which superstition, in league with tyranny, had enveloped it.

We shall show how these flaws in the educational system, the variety of religious beliefs, the diversity of forms of government placed obstacles of differing degrees of seriousness in the way of the progress of the human mind. It will be shown that this progress became increasingly slow as the problems studied verged upon the province of political and religious interests, so that general philosophy and metaphysics, whose truths directly attacked all superstitious beliefs, encountered far more obstinate resistance than political science, whose advance threatened only the authority of kings or aristocratic senates; and a similar state of affairs can be observed in the progress of the physical sciences.

We shall expatiate upon the ways in which the progress of every science has been affected by the nature of the subject that it studies or of the methods that it employs.

It can be similarly observed how the same science has been differently affected in different countries by the political and natural causes at work. As far as these differences are concerned we shall try to estimate the influence of differences in religion, in the form of government, in the wealth and power of the nation, in its character and geographical position, and in the various events of its history. Finally, we shall take into consideration the work of chance in blessing a particular country with one or more of those outstanding men whose influence, while it extends over the whole of humanity, is felt more powerfully within their own nation.

We shall distinguish between the progress of science itself which can be measured only by the number of known truths, and the progress of a nation in each science, which is to be measured partly in terms of the number of people who are familiar with the more obvious and more important truths and partly in terms of the number and nature of these truths. We have indeed arrived at that point of civilization where the mass of the people profit from knowledge not only through what they owe to the more enlightened members of their community but through the uses to which they themselves put it, in defending themselves against error, in anticipating or satisfying their needs, in preserving themselves from the troubles of life or in mitigating them by new pleasures.

The history of the persecution to which the defenders of truth were exposed at this time will not be forgotten. We shall see how such persecution extended from philosophical or political truths to those of medicine, natural history, physics and astronomy. In the eighth century an ignorant pope had persecuted a deacon for having upheld that the earth was round contrary to the opinion of the rhetorician Augustine; in the seventeenth the far more shameful ignorance of another pope handed Galileo over to the inquisition on the ground that he had proved the daily and yearly movement of the earth. The greatest genius whom modern Italy gave to science, bowed down by illness and infirmity, was obliged under threat of torture and prison to ask God's forgiveness for having led men to a better knowledge of his works and for having taught them how to admire him in the simplicity of the eternal laws by which he governs the universe. Yet the absurdity of the theologians was so palpable that they had to yield to human understanding and permit the belief that the earth moved, provided that it was a *hypothesis* and that faith was not thereby attacked. But the astronomers did precisely the opposite; they believed in the real movement of the earth and calculated it on the *hypothesis* of its immobility.

Three great men have marked the transition from this stage of history to the next: Bacon, Galileo, Descartes.

Bacon revealed the true method of studying nature and of using the three instruments that she has given us for penetrating her secrets; observation, experience and calculation. He asked that the philosopher, cast into the middl of the universe, should begin by renouncing all the belie. that he had received and even all the notions he had formed, so that he might then recreate for himself, as it were, a new understanding admitting only of precise ideas, accurate notions and truths whose degree of certainty or probability had been strictly weighed. But Bacon, who possessed the genius of philosophy in the highest degree, was without the genius of science; and these methods for discovering truth, of which he gave no examples, were admired by philosophers but in no way influenced the course of science.

Galileo enriched the sciences by useful and brilliant

discoveries. He showed by example how to arrive at a knowledge of the laws of nature by a sure and fruitful method, which did not necessitate sacrificing the hope of success to the fear of error. He founded the first school in which the sciences were studied without any admixture of superstition in favour of either popular prejudices or authority, and where all methods other than experiment and calculation were rejected with philosophical severity. But in limiting himself exclusively to the mathematical and physical sciences, he could not afford mankind that general guidance of which it seemed to stand in need.

This honour was reserved for Descartes, a bold and clever philosopher. Endowed with great genius for the sciences, he joined example to precept and gave a method for finding and recognizing truth. He showed how to apply this in his discovery of the laws of dioptrics and the laws of the collision of bodies and finally in the development of a new branch of mathematics which was to move forward the frontiers of the subject.

He wished to extend his method to all the subjects of human thought; God, man and the universe were in turn the objects of his meditations. If his progress in the physical sciences was less certain than Galileo's, if his philosophy was less wise than Bacon's, if he can be reproached with not having learnt sufficiently from the precepts of the one and the practice of the other, to distrust his imagination, to ask questions of nature only by experiment, to believe only in calculation and the observation of the universe instead of fashioning it, to study man instead of speculating about him, still the very audacity of his mistakes served to further the progress of the human race. He stimulated men's minds, and this all the wisdom of his rivals had never done. He commanded men to shake off the yoke of authority, to recognize none save that which was avowed by reason; and he was obeyed, because he won men by his boldness and led them by his enthusiasm.

The human mind was not yet free but it knew that it was formed to be so. Those who dared to insist that it should be kept in its old chains or to try and impose new ones upon it, were forced to show why it should submit to them; and from that day onwards it was certain that they would soon be broken.

THE NINTH STAGE

From Descartes to the foundation of the French Republic

WE have watched man's reason being slowly formed by the natural progress of civilization; we have watched superstition seize upon it and corrupt it, and tyranny degrade and deaden the minds of men under the burden of misery and fear.

One nation alone escapes the two-fold influence of tyranny and superstition. From that happy land where freedom had only recently kindled the torch of genius, the mind of man, released from the leading-strings of its infancy, advances with firm steps towards the truth. But this triumph soon encourages tyranny to return, followed by its faithful companion superstition, and the whole of mankind is plunged once more into darkness, which seems as if it must last for ever. Yet, little by little, day breaks again; eyes long condemned to darkness catch a glimpse of the light and close again, then slowly become accustomed to it, and at last gaze on it without flinching; once again genius dares to walk abroad on the earth, from which fanaticism and barbarism had exiled it.

We have already seen reason lift her chains, shake herself free from some of them, and, all the time regaining strength, prepare for and advance the moment of her liberation. It remains for us to study the stage in which she finally succeeds in breaking these chains, and when, still compelled to drag their vestiges behind her, she frees herself from them one by one; when at last she can go forward unhindered,

THE NINTH STAGE 125

and the only obstacles in her path are those that are inevitably renewed at every fresh advance because they are the necessary consequence of the very constitution of our understanding—of the connection, that is, between our means of discovering the truth and the resistance that it offers to our efforts.

Religious intolerance had forced seven of the Belgian provinces to throw off the yoke of Spain and form a federal republic. Religious intolerance alone had aroused the spirit of English liberty, which, exhausted by a protracted and bloody civil war, was finally embodied in a constitution that was for long the admiration of philosophers, but owes its preservation merely to the superstition of the English nation and the hypocrisy of their politicians. And, finally, it was also through priestly persecution that the Swedish nation found courage to reclaim a portion of their rights.

However, in the midst of all these advances, which owed their origin to theological disputes, France, Spain, Hungary and Bohemia saw their feeble liberties extinguished, or so at least it seemed.

It would be vain to look, in those countries which we call free, for that liberty which infringes none of the natural rights of man; a liberty which not only allows man to possess these rights but allows him to exercise them. For the liberty we find there is based on a system of positive rights, unequally distributed among men, and grants them different privileges according to the town in which they live, the class into which they have been born, the means of which they can dispose, and the profession that they follow. A comparative sketch of the curious inequalities to be found in different countries is the best retort that we can make to those who still uphold their virtue or necessity.

But in these same countries the law guarantees individual and civil liberty, so that if man has not there reached a state of perfection, his natural dignity is not degraded; some at

least of his rights are recognized; he can no longer be said to
be a slave though he can be said to be not truly free.

In those nations where at this time there was, to a greater
or less extent, a genuine loss of liberty, the political rights
enjoyed by the great mass of the people had been confined
within such narrow limits that the destruction of the virtually
arbitrary power of the aristocracy under which man had
groaned, seems to have more than compensated for their
loss. Man lost the title of citizen, which inequality had
rendered little more than a name, but the quality of man
was accorded greater respect; royal despotism saved him
from feudal oppression, and relieved him from a state of
humiliation all the more painful because the awareness
of his condition was constantly kept alive in him by
the number and actual presence of his tyrants. The
system of laws tended to improve, both in those states
whose constitution was partly free, and in those ruled by
despots: in the former because the interests of those who
exercised the real power did not invariably conflict with the
interests of the people; in the latter because the interests
of the despot were often indistinguishable from those of
public prosperity, or because the despot's endeavours to
destroy the vestiges of feudal or clerical power had imparted
to the law a spirit of equality, whose inspiration may have
been the desire to establish equality in slavery, but whose
effects were often salutary.

We shall give a detailed exposition of the causes that have
produced in Europe a kind of despotism for which there is
no precedent in earlier ages or in other parts of the world,
a despotism in which an all but arbitrary authority, restrained by public opinion, controlled by enlightenment,
tempered by self-interest, has often contributed to the
progress of wealth, industry, and education, and sometimes
even to that of liberty.

Manners have become less violent through the weaken-
ing of the prejudices that had maintained their savagery,

through the influence of the spirit of industry and commerce which is inimical to unrest and violence as the natural enemies of wealth, through the sense of horror inspired by the none too distant picture of the barbarism of the preceding stage, through a wider diffusion of the philosophical ideas of equality and humanity, and, finally, through the influence, slow but sure, of the general progress of enlightenment.

Religious intolerance remains, but more as an instrument of human prudence, as a tribute to popular prejudice, or as a precaution against popular unrest. Its fury abates; the fires at the stake are seldom lit, and have been replaced by a form of oppression that, if it is often more arbitrary, is less barbarous; and of recent years the persecutions have become much rarer, and the result rather of complacency or habit. Everywhere, and in every respect, governmental practice has slowly and regretfully followed the progress of public opinion and even of philosophy.

Indeed, if in the moral and political sciences there is always a large interval between the point to which philosophers have carried the progress of enlightenment and the degree of enlightenment attained by the average man of education (and it is the body of beliefs held in common by such men that constitutes the generally accepted creed known as public opinion), those who direct public affairs and who immediately influence the fate of the common people, under whatever constitution they may hold their powers, are very far from rising to the level of public opinion; they follow its advance, without ever overtaking it and are always many years behind it and therefore always ignorant of many of the truths that it has learned.

This sketch of the progress of philosophy and of the dissemination of enlightenment, whose more general and more evident effects we have already examined, brings us up to the stage when the influence of progress upon public opinion, of public opinion upon nations or their leaders, suddenly ceases to be a slow, imperceptible affair, and produces a revolution in the whole order of several nations, a certain earnest of the revolution that must one day include in its scope the whole of the human race.

After long periods of error, after being led astray by vague or incomplete theories, publicists have at last discovered the true rights of man and how they can all be deduced from the single truth, that *man is a sentient being, capable of reasoning and of acquiring moral ideas.*

They have seen that the maintenance of these rights was the sole object of men's coming together in political societies, and that the social art is the art of guaranteeing the preservation of these rights and their distribution in the most equal fashion over the largest area. It was felt that in every society the means of assuring the rights of the individual should be submitted to certain common rules, but that the authority to choose these means and to determine these rules could belong only to the majority of the members of the society itself; for in making this choice the individual cannot follow his own reason without subjecting others to it, and the will of the majority is the only mark of truth that can be accepted by all without loss of equality.

Each man can in fact genuinely bind himself in advance to the will of the majority which then becomes unanimous; but he can bind only himself; and he cannot engage even himself towards this majority when it fails to respect the rights of the individual, after having once recognized them.

Here we see at once the rights of the majority over society or its members, and the limits of these rights. Here we see the origin of that unanimity which allows the decisions taken by the majority alone to impose an obligation upon all; an obligation which ceases to be legitimate when, with a change in the individuals constituting the majority, the sanction of unanimity no longer exists. Doubtless there are issues on which the decision of the majority is likely to be in favour of error and against the interests of all: but it is still this majority that must decide which issues are not to be

subjected to its own direct decision; it is the majority that
must appoint those persons whose judgment it considers to
be more reliable than its own; it is the majority that must
lay down the procedure that it considers most likely to
conduct them to the truth; and it may not abdicate its
authority to decide whether the decisions they take on
its behalf do or do not infringe the rights that are common
to all.

So, in the face of such simple principles, we see the
disappearance of the belief in the existence of a contract
between the people and their lawgivers, which can be
annulled only by mutual consent or by the defection of one
of the parties; and along with it there disappeared the less
servile but no less absurd opinion according to which a
nation was for ever chained to its constitution once this
constitution had been established—as though the right to
change it were not the guarantee of every other right, and as
though human institutions, which are necessarily defective
and capable of perfection as men become more enlightened,
could be condemned to remain for ever in their infancy.
Man was thus compelled to abandon that astute and false
policy, which, forgetful of the truth that all men possess
equal rights by nature, would seek to apportion those rights
unequally between countries, according to the character or
prosperity of a country, the conditions of its industry and
commerce, and unequally between men, according to a
man's birth, fortune, or profession, and which then calls
into being conflicting interests and opposing forces to
restore the balance, measures which would have been
unnecessary without this policy and which are in any event
impotent to control its more dangerous tendencies.

Nor did men any longer dare to divide humanity into two
races, the one fated to rule, the other to obey, the one to
deceive, the other to be deceived. They had to recognize
that all men have an equal right to be informed on all that
concerns them, and that none of the authorities established

K

by men over themselves has the right to hide from them one
single truth.

These principles, which the noble Sydney paid for with
his blood and on which Locke set the authority of his name,
were later developed by Rousseau with greater precision,
breadth and energy, and he deserves renown for having
established them among the truths that it is no longer
permissible to forget or to combat. Man has certain needs
and also certain faculties with which to satisfy them; from
these faculties and from their products, modified and distributed in different ways, there results an accumulation of
wealth out of which must be met the common needs of
mankind. But what are the laws according to which this
wealth is produced or distributed, accumulated or con-
sumed, increased or dissipated? What, too, are the laws
governing that general tendency towards an equilibrium
between supply and demand from which it follows that,
with any increase in wealth, life becomes easier and men
are happier, until a point is reached when no further
increase is possible; or that, again, with any decrease in
wealth, life becomes harder, suffering increases, until the
consequent fall in population restores the balance? How,
with all the astonishing multifariousness of labour and production, supply and demand, with all the frightening complexity of conflicting interests that link the survival and
well-being of one individual to the general organization of
societies, that make his well-being dependent on every
accident of nature and every political event, his pain and
pleasure on what is happening in the remotest corner of
the globe, how, with all this seeming chaos, is it that, by a
universal moral law, the efforts made by each individual on
his own behalf minister to the welfare of all, and that the
interests of society demand that everyone should understand
where his own interests lie, and should be able to follow
them without hindrance?

Men, therefore, should be able to use their faculties,

dispose of their wealth and provide for their needs in complete freedom. The common interest of any society, far from demanding that they should restrain such activity, on the contrary, forbids any interference with it; and as far as this aspect of public order is concerned, the guaranteeing to each man his natural rights is at once the whole of social utility, the sole duty of the social power, the only right that the general will can legitimately exercise over the individual.

But it is not enough merely that this principle should be acknowledged by society; the public authority has specific duties to fulfil. It must establish by law recognized measures for the determination of the weight, volume, size and length of all articles of trade; it must create a coinage to serve as a common measure of value and so to facilitate comparison between the value of one article of trade and that of another, so that having a value itself, it can be exchanged against anything else that can be given one; for without this common measure trade must remain confined to barter, and can acquire very little activity or scope.

The wealth produced each year provides a portion for disposal which is not required to pay for either the labour that has produced it or the labour required to ensure its replacement by an equal or greater production of wealth. The owner of this disposable portion does not owe it directly to his work; he possesses it independently of the use to which he puts his faculties in order to provide for his needs. Hence it is out of this available portion of the annual wealth that the public authority, without violating anyone's rights, can establish the funds required for the security of the State, the preservation of peace within its borders, the protection of individual rights, the exercise of those powers established for the formation or execution of the law, and, finally, the maintenance of public prosperity.

There are certain undertakings and institutions which are beneficial to society in general, and which it therefore ought to initiate, control and supervise; these provide services which the wishes and interests of individuals cannot provide by themselves, and which advance the progress of agriculture, industry or trade or the prevention or alleviation of inevitable natural hardships or unforeseen accidents.

Up to the stage of which we speak and even for a long time afterwards, these various undertakings were left to chance, to the greed of governments, to the skill of charlatans or to the prejudices or self-interest of powerful sections of the community. A disciple of Descartes, however, the famous and ill-starred John de Witt, felt that political economy ought like every other science to submit itself to the principles of philosophy and the rigour of calculation.

Political economy made little progress until the Peace of Utrecht gave Europe the promise of lasting peace. From then onwards one notices an increasing intellectual interest taken in this hitherto neglected subject; and the new science was advanced by Stewart, Smith and more particularly the French economists, at least as far as precision and the purity of its principles are involved, to a point that one could hardly have hoped to reach so soon after such a long period of indifference.

But this progress in politics and political economy was caused primarily by the progress in general philosophy and metaphysics, if we take the latter word in its broadest sense.

Descartes had brought philosophy back to reason; for he had understood that it must be derived entirely from those primary and evident truths which we can discover by observing the operations of the human mind. Soon, however, his impatient imagination snatched it from the path that he had traced for it, and for a time it seemed that philosophy had regained her independence only to be led astray by new errors.

At last, Locke grasped the thread by which philosophy should be guided; he showed that an exact and precise analysis of ideas, which reduces them step by step to other ideas of more immediate origin or of simpler composition, is the only way to avoid being lost in that chaos of incomplete, incoherent and indeterminate notions which chance presents to us at hazard and we unthinkingly accept.

By this same analysis he proved that all ideas are the result of the operations of our minds upon sensations we have received, or, to put it more exactly, that they are the combinations of these sensations presented to us simultaneously by the faculty of memory in such a way that our attention is arrested and our perception is thereby limited to no more than a part of such compound sensations.

He showed that if we attach a word to each idea after analysing it and circumscribing it, we shall succeed in remembering the idea ever afterwards in a uniform fashion; that is to say, the idea will always be formed of the same simple ideas, it will always be enclosed within the same limits, and it can in consequence be used in a chain of reasoning without any risk of confusion. On the other hand, if a word is used in such a way that it does not correspond to a determinate idea, it can at different times arouse different ideas in the same person's mind, and this is the most fecund source of error in reasoning.

Locke, finally, was the first man who dared to set a limit to the human understanding, or rather to determine the nature of the truths that it can come to know and of the objects it can comprehend.

This method was soon adopted by all philosophers and, by applying it to moral science, to politics and to social economy, they were able to make almost as sure progress in these sciences as they had in the natural sciences. They were able to admit only proven truths, to separate these truths from whatever as yet remained doubtful and uncertain, and to ignore whatever is and always will be impossible to know.

[Similarly the analysis of our feelings, leads to our finding, in the development of our capacity to feel pleasure and pain, the origin of our moral ideas, the foundation of those general truths which, resulting from these ideas, determine the necessary and immutable laws of justice and injustice, and, finally, the motives that we have for conforming to them, motives which spring from the very nature of our sensibility, from what might be called our moral constitution.]

This metaphysical method became virtually a universal instrument. Men learnt to use it in order to perfect the methods of the physical sciences, to throw light on their principles and to examine the validity of their proofs; and it was extended to the examination of facts and to the rules of taste.

Thus it was applied to all the various undertakings of the human understanding, and by means of it the operations of the mind in every branch of knowledge were subjected to analysis, and the nature of the truths and the kind of certainty we can expect to find from each of these branches of knowledge was thereby revealed. It is this new step in philosophy that has for ever imposed a barrier between mankind and the errors of its infancy, a barrier that should save it from relapsing into its former errors under the influence of new prejudices, just as it should assure the eventual eradication of those that still survive unrecognized, and should make it certain that any that may take their place will exercise only a faint influence and enjoy only an ephemeral existence.

In Germany, however, a man of vast and profound genius laid the foundations of a new doctrine. His ardent and passionate imagination could not rest satisfied with a modest philosophy and leave unsolved those great questions about the spirituality or the survival of the human soul, about man's freedom or the freedom of God, about the existence of pain and evil in a universe governed by an all-powerful intelligence whose wisdom, justice and loving-kindness ought, it would seem, to exclude the possibility of their existence. He cut the knot which the most skilful analysis would never have been able to untie and constructed the universe from simple, indestructible, entities equal by their very nature. The relations of each of these entities with all the others, which with it form part of the system of the universe, determine those qualities of it whereby it differs from every other. The human soul and the least atom of a block of stone are, each of them, one of these monads, and they differ only in the different place assigned to them in the universal order. Out of all the possible combinations of these beings an infinite intelligence has preferred one, and could have preferred one only, the most perfect of all. If that which exists offends us by the misery and crime that we see in it, it is still true that any other combination would have had more painful results.

We shall explain this system which, being adopted, or at least upheld, by Leibniz's compatriots, has retarded the progress of philosophy amongst them. One entire school of English philosophers enthusiastically embraced and eloquently defended the doctrine of optimism, but they were less subtle and less profound than Leibniz, for whereas he based his doctrine on the belief that an all-powerful intelligence, by the very necessity of its nature, could choose only the best of all possible worlds, the English philosophers sought to prove their doctrine by appealing to observation of the particular world in which we live and, thereby sacrificing all the advantages possessed by this system so long as it remains abstract and general; they lost themselves in details, which were too often either revolting or ridiculous.

In Scotland, however, other philosophers finding that the analysis of the development of our actual faculties led to no principle that could provide a sufficiently pure or solid basis for the morality of our actions, thought to attribute a hew faculty to the human soul, distinct from but associated with those of feeling or thinking, a faculty whose existence they proved only by showing that they could not do without it.

We shall recount the history of these opinions and shall show how, if they have retarded the progress of philosophy, they have advanced the dissemination of philosophical ideas.

Up till now we have shown the progress of philosophy only in the men who have cultivated, deepened and perfected it. It remains for us to show what have been its effects on public opinion; how reason, while it learnt to safeguard itself against the errors into which the imagination and respect for authority had so often led it, at last found a sure method of discovering and recognizing truth; and how at the same time it destroyed the prejudices of the masses which had for so long afflicted and corrupted the human race.

At last man could proclaim aloud his right, which for so long had been ignored, to submit all opinions to his own reason and to use in the search for truth the only instrument for its recognition that he has been given. Every man learnt with a sort of pride that nature had not for ever condemned him to base his beliefs on the opinions of others; the superstitions of antiquity and the abasement of reason before the transports of supernatural religion disappeared from society as from philosophy.

Soon there was formed in Europe a class of men who were concerned less with the discovery or development of the truth than with its propagation, men who whilst devoting themselves to the tracking down of prejudices in the hiding places where the priests, the schools, the governments and all long-established institutions had gathered and protected them, made it their life-work to destroy popular errors rather than to drive back the frontiers of human knowledge —an indirect way of aiding its progress which was not less fraught with peril, nor less useful.

In England Collins and Bolingbroke, in France Bayle, Fontenelle, Voltaire, Montesquieu and the schools founded by these famous men, fought on the side of truth, using in turn all the weapons with which learning, philosophy, wit

and literary talent can furnish reason; using every mood
from humour to pathos, every literary form from the vast
erudite encyclopædia to the novel or the broadsheet of the
day; covering truth with a veil that spared weaker eyes and
excited one to guess what lay beyond it; skilfully flattering
prejudices so as to attack them the better; seldom threaten-
ing them, and then always either only one in its entirety or
several partially; sometimes conciliating the enemies of
reason by seeming to wish only for a half-tolerance in
religious matters, only for a half-freedom in politics; sparing
despotism when tilting against the absurdities of religion,
and religion when abusing tyranny; yet always attacking
the principles of these two scourges even when they seemed
to be against only their more revolting or ridiculous abuses,
and laying their axes to the very roots of these sinister trees
when they appeared to be lopping off a few stray branches;
sometimes teaching the friends of liberty that superstition
is the invincible shield behind which despotism shelters
and should therefore be the first victim to be sacrificed,
the first chain to be broken, and sometimes denouncing it
to the despots as the real enemy of their power, and
frightening them with stories of its secret machinations and
its bloody persecutions; never ceasing to demand the
independence of reason and the freedom of the press as the
right and the salvation of mankind; protesting with inde-
fatigable energy against all the crimes of fanaticism and
tyranny; pursuing, in all matters of religion, administration,
morals and law, anything that bore the marks of tyranny,
harshness or barbarism; invoking the name of nature to bid
kings, captains, magistrates and priests to show respect for
human life; laying to their charge, with vehemence and
severity, the blood their policy or their indifference still
spilled on the battlefield or on the scaffold; and finally,
taking for their battle cry—*reason, tolerance, humanity.*

Such was the new philosophy: an object of common
hatred to all those many sections of society which owe their

existence to prejudice, their survival to error, their power to credulity; welcomed nearly everywhere, but persecuted none the less; numbering kings, priests, great men and lawyers among its disciples and among its enemies. Its leaders, were in general, astute enough to escape vengeance, although exposing themselves to hatred; and to hide from persecution, though remaining sufficiently in evidence to lose none of the glory.

A government would often reward them with one hand, and pay their slanderers with the other; proscribe them, and feel honoured that they had been born on their soil; punish their opinions, and yet feel humiliated if they were suspected of not sharing them.

These opinions were to become those of all enlightened men, professed by some, dissimulated by others, with a hypocrisy whose transparency varied with their strength or timidity of character, and which was dependent on whether they yielded to the interests of their profession or to those of their vanity. But already the interests of vanity were so strong, that, in place of the profound dissimulation of preceding ages, men were content with a prudent reserve for themselves and often even in others.

We shall trace the progress of this philosophy in different parts of Europe where it was soon rapidly diffused, despite governmental and priestly inquisitions, by the almost universal medium of the French language. We shall show how skilful policy and superstition recruited against it every motive for mistrusting reason that human ingenuity could suggest, every argument that demonstrated its weakness and its limitations, and how people contrived to employ even total scepticism in the service of credulity.

That simple system which regarded the enjoyment of an unlimited freedom as the surest encouragement to trade and industry; which delivered the masses from the destructive scourge and humiliating yoke of taxes unjustly imposed, and extravagantly and often cruelly raised, and substituted

for them just, equal, and almost imperceptible contributions;
which linked the state's true power and wealth to the well-
being of the individual and a respect for his rights; which
bound together in bonds of mutual happiness the different
classes into which societies are naturally divided; which
preached the comforting doctrine of the brotherhood of
man, whose gentle harmony should no longer be upset by
the self-interest of nations: all these principles, attractive
on account of their nobility, simplicity and breadth of
vision, were propagated enthusiastically by the French
economists. Their success was less prompt and less general
than that of the philosophers, for the prejudices they had
to fight were less crude, and the errors subtler. They had to
enlighten before they could disabuse of error, and to teach
common sense before they could employ it as an arbiter.

If, however, they were able to win only a small number
of converts to their doctrine in its entirety, if people were
frightened of the universality of their maxims and the
inflexibility of their principles, and if they themselves
harmed their cause by affecting an obscure and dogmatic
manner of exposition, by appearing to favour free trade at
the expense of political liberty and by presenting in too
magisterial and dogmatic a fashion certain parts of their
system that they had insufficiently investigated, at least
they succeeded in showing how odious and despicable were
those cowardly, crafty and corrupt political doctrines which
looked for the prosperity of a nation in the impoverishment
of its neighbours, in the short-sighted policy of a protec-
tionist regime and in the petty calculations of a tyrannical
exchequer.

The salutary influence of the new truths with which genius
had enriched philosophy, politics and public economy,
and which had been adopted more or less generally by
enlightened men, was felt far afield.

The art of printing had spread so widely and had so
greatly increased the number of books published; the books

that were published catered so successfully for every degree
of knowledge, or industry, or income; they were so pro-
portioned to every taste, or cast of mind; they presented
such easy and often such pleasant means of instruction;
they opened so many doors to truth that it was no longer
possible that they should all of them be closed again, that
there was no class and no profession from which the truth
could be withheld. And so, though there remained a great
number of people condemned to ignorance either voluntary
or enforced, the boundary between the cultivated and the
uncultivated had been almost entirely effaced, leaving an
insensible gradation between the two extremes of genius
and stupidity.

Thus, an understanding of the natural rights of man, the
belief that these rights are inalienable and indefeasible, a
strongly expressed desire for liberty of thought and letters,
of trade and industry, and for the alleviation of the people's
suffering, for the proscription of all penal laws against
religious dissenters and the abolition of torture and barbarous punishments, the desire for a milder system of
criminal legislation and jurisprudence which should give
complete security to the innocent, and for a simpler civil
code, more in conformance with reason and nature, indifference in all matters of religion which now were relegated
to the status of superstitions and political impostures, a
hatred of hypocrisy and fanaticism, a contempt for prejudice, zeal for the propagation of enlightenment: all these
principles, gradually filtering down from philosophical
works to every class of society whose education went
beyond the catechism and the alphabet, became the common faith, the badges of all those who were neither Machia-
vellians nor fools. In some countries these principles formed
a public opinion sufficiently widespread for even the mass
of the people to show a willingness to be guided by it and
to obey it. For a feeling of humanity, a tender and active
compassion for all the misfortunes that afflict the human

race and a horror of anything that in the actions of public
institutions, or governments, or individuals, adds new pains
to those that are natural and inevitable, were the natural
consequences of those principles; and this feeling exhaled
from all the writings and all the speeches of the time, and
already its happy influence had been felt in the laws and the
public institutions, even of those nations still subject to
despotism.

The philosophers of different nations who considered the
interests of the whole of humanity without distinction of
country, race, or creed, formed a solid phalanx banded
together against all forms of error, against all manifestations
of tyranny, despite their differences in matters of theory.
Activated by feelings of universal philanthropy, they fought
injustice even when it occurred in countries other than their
own and could not harm them personally; they fought injustice even when it was their own country that was guilty of
acts against others; they raised an outcry in Europe against
the crimes of greed that sullied the shores of America,
Africa, and Asia. English and French philosophers considered themselves honoured to be called the *friends* of the
black races whom their foolish tyrants disdained to consider
as members of the human race. In France writers lavished
enconiums on the new-won tolerance accorded in Russia
and Sweden: whilst in Italy Beccaria denounced the barbarous tenets of French jurisprudence. In France writers
sought to free England from her commercial prejudices and
her superstitious respect for the vices of her constitution
and her laws, whilst the worthy Howard denounced to the
French the callous indifference which was causing the
death of so many human victims in their prison-cells and
hospitals.

Force or persuasion on the part of governments, priestly
intolerance, and even national prejudices, had all lost their
deadly power to smother the voice of truth, and nothing
could now protect the enemies of reason or the oppressors

of freedom from a sentence to which the whole of Europe would soon subscribe.

Finally, we see the rise of a new doctrine which was to deal the final blow to the already tottering structure of prejudice—the doctrine of the indefinite perfectibility of the human race of which Turgot, Price and Priestley were the first and the most brilliant apostles. This doctrine belongs to the tenth stage of our history, and there we shall examine it in greater detail. But here we must describe the origin and the progress of a false philosophy against which the support of that doctrine is so necessary if reason is to triumph.

Born of pride in some and of self-interest in others, conniving at the perpetuation of ignorance and the continued reign of error, it has had its numerous adherents ready to corrupt men's reason with brilliant paradoxes or to lull it into the comfortable indolence of absolute Pyrrhonism; so to despise the human race as to teach it that the progress of knowledge would be not only useless but dangerous both to its happiness and to its freedom; ready to infuse it with a false enthusiasm and grandiose illusions about a new species of wisdom that would absolve virtue from the need of enlightenment and common sense from the verdict of fact; ready, on the one hand, to speak of philosophy and the sciences as subjects too arduous for a mere human being with limited powers, at the mercy of his wants, weighed down with the pressing cares of daily life; and, on the other, to pour scorn on these sciences as a heap of uncertain and extravagant speculations, and to maintain that in all matters the skill, the practical experience of the statesman should be preferred to them. The adherents of this philosophy chose the moment when knowledge was progressing more rapidly than ever before, to complain incessantly of its decline; the moment when men were at last beginning to remember their rights and to employ their reason, to deplore the degeneration of mankind: they even went so far as to predict that by a swing of the pendulum mankind was

about to plunge once more into barbarism, ignorance, and
slavery, just when everything combined to show that men
had left these evils behind them for ever. Indeed, it seemed
that they were either humiliated by the progress of mankind
because they had made no contribution towards it, or
terrified because it presaged their fall from power and
importance. [Moreover, some charlatans, less foolish than
those who were still clumsily trying to shore up the fabric
of ancient superstitions whose foundations had been undermined by philosophy, endeavoured to construct out of their
ruins a religious system in which reason would be called
upon to make only a partial submission and would remain
free to believe what she wished, so long as she consented
to believe something incomprehensible. Others tried
through secret societies to revive the forgotten mysteries
of ancient theurgy; abandoning the masses to their errors
while chaining their disciples in new superstitions, they
had the audacity to hope that they might bring back, for the
benefit of a few initiates, the ancient tyranny of the pontiff
kings of India and Egypt. But philosophy, resting on the unshakable foundations prepared for her by science, opposed
to their attempts a wall against which they broke in vain.]

A comparison of the attitude of mind I have already
described with the forms of government prevalent at that
time would have made it easy to foresee that a great revolution was inevitable, and that there were only two ways in
which it could come about; either the people themselves
would establish the reasonable and natural principles that
philosophy had taught them to admire, or governments
would hasten to anticipate them and carry out what was
required by public opinion. If the revolution should come
about in the former way it would be swifter and more
thorough, but more violent; if it should come about in the
latter way, it would be less swift and less thorough, but also
less violent: if in the former way, then freedom and happiness would be purchased at the price of transient evils; if

in the latter, then these evils would be avoided but, it might be, at the price of long delaying the harvest of the fruits that the revolution must, nevertheless, inevitably bear. The ignorance and corruption of the governments of the time saw that it came about in the former way, and the human race was avenged by the swift triumph of liberty and reason.

Simple common sense taught the inhabitants of the British colonies that Englishmen born beyond the Atlantic Ocean had been endowed by nature with exactly the same rights as other Englishmen born under the meridian of Greenwich, and that a difference of 70 degrees of longitude was not enough to change these rights. They had, perhaps, a better idea than most Europeans of what were the rights common to every member of the human race and amongst them they included the right not to pay taxes without consent. But the British government affected to believe that God had created America, as he had created Asia, for the pleasure of the inhabitants of London; for it wanted to have in its power a vassal nation beyond the seas that, when the time came, could be used to crush revolt in England. It therefore ordered the compliant representatives of the English people to violate the rights of America, and to impose taxation on her without asking her consent. America proclaimed that this injustice released her from the obligations binding her to England, and she declared her independence.

We see then for the first time, a great people delivered from all its chains, giving itself in peace the laws and the constitution that it believed most likely to bring it happiness. Its geographical situation and its old political form obliging it to form a federal republic, there were at once set up thirteen republican constitutions, each based on a solemn recognition of the natural rights of man, and having for its chief end the preservation of these rights. We shall sketch the form of these constitutions, and show how much they owed to the progress of the political sciences; and we shall show how they were tainted with the prejudices that those who drafted them had imbibed in their youth: how, for example, their simplicity was impaired by the determination to preserve a balance of power within the state, and how they had as their principle the identity of interests rather than the equality of rights. We shall demonstrate not only that this principle of the identity of interests, once made the basis for political rights, is a violation of the rights of those who are thereby debarred from a complete exercise of them, but also that this identity ceases to exist once it gives rise to genuine inequality. We shall insist on this point because the fallacy involved in accepting this principle is the only one still likely to be dangerous, since it is the only one to which intelligent men are not yet wholly alive. We shall show how the American republics put into practice the idea, which was still new even in theory, of the necessity for establishing by law a regular and peaceful procedure for reforming the constitution itself, and of distinguishing the authority entrusted with such reforms from the ordinary legislative authority.

But in the war that arose between two enlightened peoples, of which one defended the natural rights of humanity whilst the other opposed to it the impious doctrine that these rights could be submitted to prescription, to political interests, to written conventions, the issue was pleaded at the bar of public opinion before the whole of Europe, and the rights of men were nobly upheld, and expounded without restriction or reserve, in writings that circulated freely from the shores of the Neva to those of the Guadalquivir. Reports of this great debate penetrated to the most oppressed countries and the most isolated settlements, and the men who lived there were astonished to hear that they had rights. They learned what they were, and they learned that other men had had the courage to defend them or to win them back.

The American revolution, then, was about to spread to

L

Europe; and if there existed a country where sympathy with the American cause had diffused more widely than elsewhere its writings and its principles, a country that was at once the most enlightened and the most enslaved of lands, a country that possessed at the same time the most enlightened philosophers and the most crassly and insolently ignorant government, a country whose laws were so far below the level of public intelligence that not even patriotism or prejudice could attach the people to its ancient institutions, was not this country destined by the very nature of things to start that revolution which the friends of humanity awaited with such impatience and such high hopes? It was inevitable, then, that the revolution should begin in France.

The maladroitness of her government precipitated it, her philosophers guided its principles and the power of her people destroyed the obstacles which might have stood in its way.

The revolution in France was more far-reaching than that in America and therefore more violent: for the Americans, who were content with the civil and criminal code that they had received from England; who had no vicious system of taxation to reform; and no feudal tyrannies, no hereditary distinctions, no rich, powerful and privileged corporations, no system of religious intolerance to destroy, limited themselves to establishing a new authority in place of that which had been exercised up till then by the British. None of these innovations affected the ordinary people or changed the relations between individuals. In France, on the contrary, the revolution was to embrace the entire economy of society, change every social relation and find its way down to the furthest links of the political chain, even down to those individuals who, living in peace on their private fortune or on the fruits of their labour, had no reason to participate in public affairs—neither opinion nor occupation nor the pursuit of wealth, power or fame.

The Americans, who gave the impression that they were fighting only against the tyrannical prejudices of the mother country, had the rivals of England as their allies; and, at the same time, other powers, jealous of her wealth and her pride, lent the support of their good will to the triumph of justice so that the whole of Europe was united against the oppressor. The French, on the contrary, attacked at once the despotism of kings, the political inequality of any constitution only partly free, the pride of the nobility, the domination, intolerance and wealth of the priesthood, and the abuses of the feudal system, all of which are still rampant in most of Europe, so that the European powers inevitably united on the side of tyranny. Consequently, all that France found raised in her favour were the voices of a few wise men, and the timid prayers of the down-trodden masses, and even this support calumny endeavoured to wrest from her.

We shall show in what ways the principles from which the constitution and laws of France were derived were purer, more precise and more profound than those that guided the Americans; how they more successfully escaped every kind of prejudice; how the equality of rights was nowhere replaced by the identity of interest, which is only a feeble and hypocritical substitute; how the theory of the limitation of powers took the place of that futile balance of powers which had so long been admired; and how for the first time in a great nation necessarily divided into a large number of isolated factions, men had the courage to allow the people to exercise their sovereign right—the right to obey only those laws the procedure for whose enactment is sanctioned by their direct assent, even if the actual enactment is delegated to their representatives, laws which, if the people should find them injurious to their interests or rights, they can revoke by the legitimate assertion of their sovereign will.

From the moment when the genius of Descartes gave men's minds that general impetus which is the first principle of a revolution in the destinies of the human race, to the happy time of complete and pure social liberty when man was able to regain his natural independence only after having lived through a long series of centuries of slavery and misery, the picture of the progress of the mathematical and physical sciences reveals an immense horizon whose different parts must be distributed and ordered if we wish to grasp the significance of the whole and properly observe its relations.

Not only did the application of algebra to geometry become a fruitful source of discoveries in these two sciences, but in proving by this great example how in general the methods of calculating magnitudes could be extended to all questions that were concerned with the measuring of extension, Descartes announced in advance that they would be applied with equal success to all the objects whose relations are capable of precision; and this great discovery, showing for the first time this final objective of the sciences, which is to subject all truths to the rigour of calculation, gave hope of reaching it and afforded a glimpse of the means towards that end.

Soon this discovery was followed by the discovery of a new calculus, showing how to find the rate of increase or decrease of a variable quantity, or to rediscover the quantity itself from the knowledge of this rate, regardless of whether one imputes a finite magnitude to this increase, or whether the rate is to be determined for a given instant—that is, when the increase is nil; a method which, as it applies to all combinations of variable magnitudes and to all hypotheses concerning their variations, also allows us to determine, for all objects whose changes are capable of precise measurement, either the relations between the elements when only those between the objects are known, or the relations between the objects when only those between the elements are known.

We owe to Newton and to Leibniz the invention of these calculi for which the work of the geometers of the previous generation had prepared the way. Their continuous progress for more than a century has been the work of several men of genius whose glory they made. They present to the eyes of the philosopher who can observe them even without being able to follow them, an imposing monument to the power of the human intelligence.

When we come to describe the formation and the principles of the language of algebra, the only really exact and analytical language yet in existence, the nature of the technical methods of this science and how they compare with the natural workings of the human understanding, we shall show that even though this method is by itself only an instrument pertaining to the science of quantities, it contains within it the principles of a universal instrument, applicable to all combinations of ideas.

Rational mechanics soon became an extensive and profound science. The true laws of the collision of bodies about which Descartes had been mistaken finally became known.

Huyghens discovered the laws of circular motion. At the same time he furnished the method of determining to what circle each element of any curve ought to belong. By combining these two theories Newton discovered the theory of curvilinear motion and applied it to those laws which Kepler had found to be followed by the planets in their elliptical orbits.

It was discovered that a planet, imagined to be projected into space at a certain moment with a certain speed and in a predetermined direction, described an ellipse round the sun by reason of a force acting upon it and inversely proportional to the square of the distance. The same force keeps the satellites in their orbits round the principal planet. And it extends to the entire system of heavenly bodies and acts reciprocally between all the elements composing them.

The regularity of planetary ellipses is disturbed by this

force and the calculus explains in detail these perturbations. It acts upon the comets for which the same theory holds, and determines their orbits and predicts their return. The movements we notice in the axes of rotation of the earth and of the moon prove once again the existence of this universal force. It is finally the cause of the weight of bodies on the earth, in which it appears to be constant because we cannot observe them at sufficiently varied distances from the centre of action.

Thus man at last discovered one of the physical laws of the universe; a law that has hitherto remained unique, like the glory of the man who revealed it.

A hundred years of labour have confirmed that law which appears to govern all celestial phenomena to a degree that is, so to say, miraculous. Every time that a phenomenon appears not to come under that law, this uncertainty soon becomes the occasion of a new triumph.

Philosophy is nearly always obliged to look into the writings of a man of genius in order to find the secret thread that guided him; but in this case, interest, inspired by admiration, has discovered and preserved some precious stories which enable us to follow Newton's progress step by step. These will be useful to us in showing how the happy conjunctions of chance combined with the efforts of genius to lead to a great discovery, and how less favourable conjunctions might have retarded them or reserved them for other hands.

But Newton perhaps did more for the progress of the human mind than discover this general law of nature; he taught men to admit in physics only precise and mathematical theories, which account not merely for the existence of a certain phenomenon but also for its quantity and extension. Nevertheless he was accused of reviving the occult qualities of the Ancients because he confined himself to locating the general cause of celestial phenomena in one simple fact, whose incontestable reality was proved by observation. And this accusation itself proves how much the methods of science still stood in need of enlightenment from philosophy.

A host of problems of statics and dynamics had been successively formulated and solved when D'Alembert discovered a general principle, which alone was enough to determine the movement of any number of particles urged by any number of forces, and related to each other by certain conditions. Soon he extended this same principle to finite bodies of a determinate figure, to those which, being elastic or flexible, could change their figure according to certain laws whilst still preserving certain relations between their parts. Finally he extended it to fluids themselves whether of a constant density or in a state of expansion. A new calculus was required for the solution of these latter questions. It could not escape his genius, and consequently mechanics was transformed into a pure calculus.

These discoveries belong to the mathematical sciences. But the nature of the law of universal gravitation and of the principles of mechanics and their consequences in so far as they reflect on the eternal order of the universe are within the province of philosophy. It was learnt that all bodies are subject to necessary laws which tend by themselves to produce or maintain equilibrium and create or preserve regularity of motion.

The knowledge of the laws that govern celestial phenomena; the discoveries of mathematical analysis, leading to more exact methods of calculating those phenomena; the perfection beyond all expectation attained by optical instruments and instruments whose precise calibration determines the precision of the observations made with their help; the precision of machines destined to measure time; the more general interest in the sciences and the concern of governments which made for an increase of astronomers and observatories—all these causes contributed to the progress of astronomy. The sky was enriched for man with new stars and he learnt how to determine and predict with exactitude their position and their movements.

Physics, having gradually delivered itself from the vague explanations introduced by Descartes, just as it had shaken off the scholastic absurdities, is now merely the art of putting nature to the question by experiment so as then to be able by calculation to deduce more general facts.

The weight of the air has been measured and found out. It was discovered that the transmission of light is not instantaneous, and its speed was measured. From this a calculation was made of the effects that should result for the apparent position of the heavenly bodies. The sun's rays were divided up into simpler light rays having different degrees of refrangibility and diversely coloured. The rainbow was explained and the means of producing its colours or making them disappear have been submitted to calculation. Electricity, which was known only as the property possessed by certain substances of attracting light bodies when rubbed, became one of the general phenomena of the universe. The cause of lightning is no longer a mystery, and Franklin has revealed to men the art of harnessing it and using it as they wish. New instruments were employed to measure variations in the weight of the atmosphere, in the humidity of the air and in the temperature of a body. A new science under the name of meteorology taught us how to understand and sometimes to predict atmospheric phenomena whose laws we shall doubtless discover one day.

In presenting the picture of these discoveries we shall show how the methods which led the physicists in their researches were purified and perfected; how the art of making experiments and of constructing instruments progressively acquired greater precision, so that physics was not only enriched day by day with new truths but the truths which had already been proved acquired greater exactitude; not only has a mass of hitherto unknown facts been observed and analysed, but all have been submitted in detail to the most rigorous methods.

Physics had had to fight only against the prejudices of scholasticism and the appeal, so seductive to idle minds, of general hypotheses. Other obstacles impeded the progress of chemistry. People had imagined that it would yield the secret of making gold and the secret of immortal life.

Great interests make for superstition. People thought that such promises, which flattered the two strongest passions of the vulgar and excited the desire for glory, could not be fulfilled by any ordinary methods, and all the extravagances that demented credulity had ever invented, seemed crammed together into the heads of chemists.

But these dreams gradually gave way to the mechanical philosophy of Descartes, which in turn was rejected and replaced by a truly experimental chemistry. Observation of the phenomena that accompany the composition and decomposition of bodies, the search for the laws governing these operations, the analysis of substances into ever simpler elements acquired an increasing precision and rigour.

But we must mention in addition to this progress in chemistry some of the improvements that, affecting, as they do, a given scientific system in its entirety by extending its methods rather than by increasing its truths, foretell and prepare a successful revolution. Such was the discovery of new methods of collecting and subjecting to experiment the expansible fluids that had hitherto eluded such examination. [This was a discovery that changed the entire system of chemistry; for it made possible control over a whole range of new entities as well as over those that were already known but had remained beyond the reach of research, and it added a new element to almost all compounds.] Another such improvement was the formation of a language in which the names designating the substances indicate either the relations or differences between those substances having a common element, or the class to which they belong. Other such improvements were the introduction of a scientific notation in which these substances are represented by analytically combined characters and that can express even the most common operations; the general laws of affinities; the use of all the methods and instruments that are employed in physics for calculating the results of experiments with rigorous precision; and finally the application of mathematics to the phenomena of crystallization and to the laws describing how the elements of certain bodies unite and take regular and constant form. Men who had for so long been satisfied with superstitions or philosophical dreams about the formation of the earth rather than proper inquiry, now at last felt the need to study, with scrupulous attention, the substances found on its surface or, where they had been led by necessity to penetrate it, in its interior, their disposition and their regular or fortuitous distribution. They learnt to recognize the marks of the slow and prolonged action of sea-water, subterranean water and fire upon it; and to distinguish those parts of the surface and external crust of the earth where the irregularities and disposition of substances, and often the substances themselves, are the work of fire, subterranean water and sea-water from other parts of the earth which have been formed for the most part from heterogeneous substances and bear the impress of earlier revolutions whose causes are still unknown to us.

Minerals, vegetables and animals are divided into several species whose members differ only in an imperceptible and irregular fashion, or for purely local causes. Several of these species resemble one another and possess a certain number of common qualities which serve to establish the successive and increasingly extensive divisions. Naturalists have learnt to classify individuals methodically according to determined characteristics which are easy to grasp, the only method of distinction possible with this innumerable multitude of different beings. These methods are a kind of real language in which every object is designated by some of its more constant qualities and by means of which, knowing these qualities, we may find the name of the object in the conventional language. These same languages, when they are well constructed, also tell us what are, for each class of natural beings, the really essential qualities whose conjunction implies a more or less complete resemblance in the remaining properties.

If we have sometimes seen men, in their pride so very conscious of the toil that the invention of these methods cost them, attach an exaggerated importance to them and take for the science itself what is merely its dictionary and its grammar, a false philosophy has also led them into the opposite excess, of holding too low an opinion of these same methods and identifying them with an arbitrary system of nomenclature, barren, painstaking compilations.

The chemical analysis of substances in the three great kingdoms of nature; the description of their external form; the exposition of their physical qualities and their ordinary properties; the history of the development of organic bodies, whether animals or plants, and of their nutrition and reproduction; the details of their organic structures; the anatomy of their different parts and the functions of each of these parts; the history of the habits of animals and of their efforts to procure food and shelter, to seize their prey or to hide from their enemies; the family or species societies which they form together; that body of truths which is attained by going through the enormous chain of natural entities; the successive links that lead from brute matter to the lowest degree of organic life, from organic matter to that which gives the first indications of spontaneous movement and sensitivity, and finally from that to man; the relations of all these entities to man, either relative to his needs or in the analogies which bring him nearer to them, or in the differences that separate him from them:—this is the picture which natural history gives us today.

Physical man has become himself the object of a separate science; *anatomy*, which in its ordinary meaning includes physiology, that science which had been retarded by a superstitious respect for the dead, profited from the general enfeeblement of prejudice and successfully undermined the support that it received from powerful men who were interested in its preservation. Its progress seems somehow to have come to a stop, and to await the discovery of improved instruments and new methods. And it now seems to be almost reduced to the study of the comparisons between the parts of animals and those of men, the organs common to different species, and the manner in which similar functions are exercised, in its search for those truths which are at the moment not open to human observation. Almost everything which the eye of the observer has been able to discover with the aid of a microscope is already unveiled. The future development of anatomy seems to depend on the possibility of experiment which has proved so useful to the progress of other sciences. But this necessary means of improvement has been denied to anatomy by the very nature of its subject.

The circulation of the blood was for long known; but the disposition of the vessels carrying the chyle which is destined to mix with it so as to make good its losses; the existence of a gastric juice which brings about the necessary decomposition of food in order to separate those parts fit to be assimilated to living fluids and organic matter; the changes that various parts and organs undergo, both in the period between conception and birth, and after birth in the different ages of life; the identification of the parts endowed with sensitivity or with that property of irritability discovered by Haller and found common to almost all organic beings—this is what physiology discovered and established by certain observation during that brilliant era; and so many important truths should secure general forgiveness for those earlier mechanical, chemical and organic explanations which have successively overburdened physiology with hypotheses baneful to the progress of science and dangerous when their application was extended to medicine.

To this picture of the sciences we must append a picture of the arts. For the arts, now resting on the sciences, made sure progress and broke the chains in which routine had hitherto bound them.

We shall show the influence that the progress of mechanics, astronomy, optics and the science of measuring time exercised over the art of building, moving and guiding ships. We shall explain how the increase in the number of observers, the greater skill of the navigator and a stricter precision in the astronomical determination of position and in topographical methods, at last laid bare the whole of the terrestrial globe which had been almost unknown at the end of the previous century; how the mechanical arts proper owed their perfection to that of the art of constructing instruments, machines and looms, and how the perfection of the latter was due to the progress of rational mechanics and of physics; we shall also show what these arts owed to the science of using existing engines with less loss and expense, and to the invention of new engines.

We shall see how architecture borrowed from the science of equilibrium and the theory of liquids, methods for making a roof that was at once less expensive and more convenient, but with no danger to the solidity of the construction; ways of resisting the impact of water in a more scientific fashion; and means of controlling its course and exploiting it by building canals with greater ingenuity and success.

We shall show how the chemical arts were enriched by new methods; and how the old methods were purified and simplified; how the useless or harmful substances, the ineffectual or imperfect practices introduced by routine were cast away; while at the same time means were discovered of preventing the terrible dangers to which workmen were often exposed, so that now they could enjoy themselves more and earn more, and no longer at a heavy price in painful sacrifice and regret.

Chemistry, botany and natural history were of use in the economic arts, and in the cultivation of useful plants; in the feeding, breeding and rearing of domestic animals; in perfecting their stocks and bettering their produce; in the preparation and conservation of the earth's supplies and animal produce.

Surgery and pharmacy have become almost new arts ever since anatomy and chemistry offered them their enlightened and certain guidance.

Medicine, which as far as its practice is concerned must be regarded as an art, was at least delivered from false theories, pedantic jargon, murderous routine, servile submission to the authority of men and the doctrine of faculties. It now teaches men to believe nothing but experience. It has increased its methods and learnt better how to combine and employ them. If in certain aspects its progress has been somewhat negative, limited to the abandonment of dangerous practices and harmful prejudices, new methods of studying chemical medicine and combining observations foretell real and far-reaching progress.

We shall above all try to follow the progress of scientific genius, which sometimes descends from a profound abstract theory to skilful and delicate applications of this theory, and, by simplifying its methods and by adapting them to our needs, extends its benefits to the most ordinary occasions; and then, at other times, stimulated by these practical needs, seeks the realm of the most elevated speculation for the assistance that was denied it by ordinary knowledge.

We shall show that declamations about the inutility of theories even in the simplest arts have never proved anything save the ignorance of those who make them. We shall point out that it is not to the profundity of these theories but on the contrary to their imperfection that we must attribute the inutility or tragic consequences of so many unfortunate applications.

These observations will lead us to this general truth, that, in all the arts, truths of theory are necessarily modified in practice; that there exist certain genuinely inevitable inexactitudes whose effects we should attempt to render nugatory without entertaining any illusory hopes of avoiding them altogether; that a great number of conditions, relating to needs, methods, time, expense, which are necessarily neglected in theory, must enter into the problem when it is a question of a real and immediate practical application; and if we consider these conditions with the true skill of practical genius, we can at once go beyond the narrow limits within which prejudice against theory threatens to constrain the arts, and also avoid the mistakes into which a clumsy application of theory might lead us.

Sciences which had been divided could not develop without closer association, without making points of contact.

Exposition of the progress within each science suffices to show what has been the utility, in several of them, of the immediate application of calculation; and how in all of them it has been used to give a greater precision both to experiment and to observation; how much they owe to mechanics, which has provided them with more perfect and more exact instruments; the extent to which the discovery of microscopes and meteorological instruments has contributed to the perfection of natural history; what this latter science owes to chemistry, which alone has been able to lead it to a deeper knowledge of the objects it deals with, to unveil for it the most intimate secrets of nature and her most essential differences, by showing the mode of composition of chemical elements; while, on the other hand, natural history provides chemistry with so many products to separate and collect, so many different operations to conduct, so many natural combinations whose true elements must be separated and whose secrets may sometimes be discovered or even imitated; and finally, physics and chemistry afford assistance to each other, and anatomy receives it so plentifully from natural history and the other sciences.

Even so we have described only a very small portion of the benefits that we have received, and are still to receive from this application. Several geometers have supplied us with general methods for finding the empirical laws of phenomena on the basis of observation, methods that can be extended to all the sciences since they lead equally to knowledge of the law giving the successive values of a given quantity for a series of moments or of positions, or the law according to which different properties, or the different values of a similar quality, are distributed between a given number of objects.

Some applications have already proved that we can successfully use the science of combinations for arranging observations in such a way as to be able to grasp more easily the relations between them, the conclusions that follow from them, and their general scheme.

The existing applications of the calculus of probability foretell how they can aid the progress of the other sciences. In some cases they can determine the probability of unusual facts and inform us whether they should be rejected or whether they deserve to be verified. In other cases they can determine the probability of the constant recurrence of those facts which often present themselves in the practice of the arts and which are not by themselves linked to an order already regarded as a general law: as, for example, in medicine the salutary results of certain remedies and the success of certain preservatives. Other applications show us what is the probability of a class of phenomena being the result of the intention of an intelligent being or of their being dependent on other preceding or coexisting phenomena; the probability too that must be attributed to that necessary and unknown cause which we call chance, a word whose true meaning can be determined only by the study of this calculus.

These applications have also taught us to recognize the different degrees of certainty that we can hope to attain; the degree of likelihood an opinion must possess before we can adopt it and use it in argument, without infringing the rights of reason or the principles of conduct, without sacrificing prudence or offending justice. They show us the advantages and disadvantages of the different systems of voting and the different ways of deciding an issue by a majority vote; the different degrees of probability that these methods produce, and for any question the degree that the public interest may rightly demand. They tell us how to determine the degree of probability with virtual certainty in cases where a decision is not necessary or where the disadvantages of the two possible courses of action are discrepant and so one of them should not be adopted as long as its chances of sucess remain below this degree of probability; or alternatively how to determine the degree of probability in advance and with complete certainty in cases where a decision is necessary and where even the slightest likelihood of its being right justifies its adoption.

We may number amongst these applications the examination of the probability of facts for those who cannot base their beliefs on their own observations—a probability which arises either from the reliability of witnesses or from the relation of the facts in question to others that have been directly observed.

The knowledge of physical man, medicine and public economy are bound to benefit from the researches about the duration of human life and the way this is influenced by differences in sex, temperature, climate, profession, government and ordinary habits; about the dependence of the death-rate on various illnesses; about changes in population, and the extent to which they depend on the action of various causes; about the distribution of population in the various countries according to age, sex and occupation.

And how useful to public economy has been the appli-

M

cation of these same calculi in the organization of life annuities, tontines, private savings banks, benefit schemes and insurance policies of every kind! Ought not the application of the calculus of probability to be applied to that part of public economy which includes the theory of measures, money, banking, financial operations, as well as taxation, its legal distribution, its actual distribution which so often contradicts the law, and its consequences for all sections of the social system?

How many important questions in this same science have been resolved only by the aid of our knowledge of natural history, agriculture, the physical constitution of plants and the mechanical or chemical arts!

Such, in a word, has been the general progress of the sciences that there is not really one of them whose principles and details can be fully developed without the help of all the others. In presenting our picture of the new truths with which each of the sciences has been enriched and of how much each owes to the application of theories or methods that seem to belong more particularly to other systems of knowledge, we shall investigate the nature and limits of the truths to which observation, experiment and meditation can lead us in each science. We shall also inquire what precisely constitutes, for each one of them, the talent of invention, that primary faculty of the human intelligence which has been given the name *genius*; by which means the mind can make the discoveries that it seeks or sometimes be led to those which it did not seek and could not even have foreseen. We shall point out how the methods which lead us to discoveries can be exhausted so that science is somehow forced to stop, unless new methods appear to provide genius with a new instrument, or to facilitate the use of those which, it seemed, could no longer be employed without waste of time and energy.

If we were to confine ourselves to showing the benefits that we have derived from the sciences in their immediate uses or in their applications to the arts, either for the well-being of individuals or for the prosperity of nations, we should display only a very small portion of their blessings.

The most important of these, perhaps, is to have destroyed prejudices and to have redirected the human intelligence, which had been obliged to follow the false directions imposed on it by the absurd beliefs that were implanted in each generation in infancy with the terrors of superstition and the fear of tyranny.

All errors in politics and morals are based on philosophical errors and these in turn are connected with scientific errors. There is not a religious system nor a supernatural extravagance that is not founded on ignorance of the laws of nature. The inventors, the defenders of these absurdities could not foresee the successive perfection of the human mind. Convinced that men in their day knew everything that they could ever know and would always believe what they then believed, they confidently supported their idle dreams on the current opinions of their country and their age.

Advances in the physical sciences are all the more fatal to these errors in that they often destroy them without appearing to attack them [, and that they can shower on those who defend them so obstinately the humiliating taunt of ignorance].

At the same time the habit of correct reasoning about the objects of these sciences, the precise ideas gained by their methods, and the means of recognizing or proving the truth of a belief should naturally lead us to compare the sentiment that forces us to accept well founded opinions credible for good reasons, with that which ties us to habitual prejudices or forces us to submit to authority. Such a comparison is enough to teach us to mistrust opinions of the latter kind, to convince us that we do not really believe them even when we boast of believing them, even when we profess them with the purest sincerity. This secret, once discovered, makes their destruction immediate and certain.

Finally this progress of the physical sciences which neither the passions nor self-interest can disturb, in which neither birth, nor profession, nor position are thought to confer on one the right to judge what one is not in a condition to understand, this inexorable progress cannot be contemplated by men of enlightenment without their wishing to make the other sciences follow the same path. It offers them at every step a model to emulate and one by which they may judge of their own efforts, recognize the false roads on which they may have set out and preserve themselves equally from pyrrhonism, from credulity, from extreme diffidence, and from a too great submission even to the authority of learning and fame.

Admittedly, metaphysical analysis led to the same results but it gave only abstract principles, while now these same abstract principles, put into practice, are illuminated by example and fortified by success.

Up to this stage, the sciences had been the birthright of very few; they were now becoming common property and the time was at hand when their elements, their principles, and their simpler methods would become truly popular. For it was then, at last, that their application to the arts and their influence on men's judgment would become of truly universal utility.

We shall follow the progress of European nations in the education both of children and of adults. This progress may appear to have been slow, if one considers only the philosophical foundations on which education has been based, for it is still in the grip of scholastic superstition: but it appears swift enough if one considers the nature and the extent of the subjects taught, for these are now confined almost completely to genuine inquiries, and include the elements of nearly all the sciences; while dictionaries, abstracts, and periodicals provide men of all ages with the information they require—even if this does not always appear in an unadulterated form. We shall examine the

utility of combining oral instruction in the sciences with
the immediate instruction to be acquired from books and
private study, and we shall also examine whether any
advantage has accrued from the development of compilation
into an accredited profession in whose practice a man may
hope to earn a livelihood; a development that has augmented
the number of indifferent books in circulation, but has also
increased the roads to knowledge open to men of little
education. We shall give an account of the influence exercised by learned societies, for these will long remain a
useful bulwark against charlatanry and false scholarship.
Finally we shall unfold the story of the encouragement given
by certain governments to the progress of knowledge, and
also of the obstacles that were laid in its path often enough by
these same governments, at the same time, in the same
country. We shall expose, on the one hand, the prejudices
and Machiavellian principles that have directed these
governments in their opposition to men's progress towards
the truth, and on the other, the political opinions originating
either from self-interest or even from a genuine concern for
the public good, that have guided them when they have
seemed interested in accelerating and protecting it.

The spectacle presented by the fine arts has no less brilliant results to show. Music has become almost a new art,
and, at the same time, its theory has been illuminated by the
application of numerical calculation to the vibration of
resonating bodies and the oscillation of the air. The graphic
arts, which had already passed from Italy to Flanders,
Spain and France, rose in the latter country to the heights
they had attained in Italy during the preceding stage, and
there shone with even greater brilliance than in Italy itself.
The art of our painters is still the art of Raphael and the
Carracci. Their methods, so far from dying out, have not
only been kept alive in the schools, but have been more
widely diffused. Nevertheless, too much time has elapsed
without the appearance of a genius comparable to Raphael

for us to attribute so long a period of sterility to chance alone. It is not that the methods of the art have been exhausted, although major achievements in it have become more difficult: it is not that nature has denied us faculties as perfect as those of the Italians of the sixteenth century; it is solely to changes in politics and in manners that we must attribute, not indeed the decadence of the art, but the feebleness of its products.

The art of letters, which, though in no way decadent in Italy, is cultivated there with less success, has made such progress in the French language that it has earned for it the honour of becoming the all but universal language of Europe. In the hands of Corneille, of Racine, of Voltaire, tragedy has risen step by step to a hitherto unknown perfection; and, in the hands of Molière, comedy has risen even more rapidly to heights as yet unattained in any other nation.

At the beginning of this period, the English language was brought to perfection, and so, more recently was the German. Both in England and in Germany, the arts of poetry and prose learned to accept, if with less docility than in France, the yoke of those universal rules of reason and of Nature which ought to be their guide. These rules are true for all languages and all peoples, although until now only very few have been capable of understanding them and of attaining that justice and certainty of taste which is merely a feeling for these rules, which presided over the works of Sophocles and Virgil as over those of Pope and Voltaire, which taught the Greeks and the Romans, as later the English and the French, to be delighted by the same beauties and to be shocked by the same faults.

We shall show what factors have favoured or impeded the progress of the arts in each nation, the reasons for the so unequal degrees of excellence attained in each nation by the various kinds of poetry and prose, and the way in which the literary rules can be modified, with no infraction of the

universal principles on which they are based, by the manners and the opinions of the nation in which a given *genre*
is practised, and by the use for which it is destined. So, for
example, tragedy intended to be spoken in daily performance,
before a small audience in a room of moderate size, cannot
have the same practical rules as tragedy intended to be sung
in an immense theatre, as part of solemn festivities to which
a whole nation is convened. We shall endeavour to prove
that the rules of taste have the same universality, the same
constancy as the other laws of the physical or the moral
universe, but are susceptible to the same kind of modification as they are when it is a question of their application in
some practical art.

We shall show how the printing press multiplies and
spreads abroad even those works primarily intended to be
performed or read aloud in public, and so allows them to
reach incomparably more people as readers than they ever
could as mere listeners; we shall show how, as a consequence
of the way that any important decision taken in a large
assembly is now determined by what the members of that
assembly have learnt through the written word, a new art
of persuasion has arisen amongst the moderns, different from
that practised by the ancients, a difference that is analogous
to the differences in the effects produced, in the means
employed between this modern art and that of the ancients;
and, finally, we shall show how in those branches of literature where even the ancients confined themselves to the
written word, such as history or philosophy, the invention
of printing makes it so much easier for the author to expand
and develop his ideas, that here again it has inevitably
modified those rules.

The progress of philosophy and the sciences has favoured
and extended the progress of letters, and this in turn has
served to make the study of the sciences easier, and that of
philosophy more popular. The sciences and the arts have
assisted one another despite the efforts of the ignorant and the

foolish to separate them and make them enemies. Scholarship, which seemed doomed by its respect for the past and its deference towards authority always to lend its support to harmful superstitions, has nevertheless contributed to their eradication, for it was able to borrow the torch of a sounder criticism from philosophy and the sciences. It already knew how to weigh up authorities and compare them; it now learned how to bring every authority before the bar of Reason. It had already discounted prodigies, fantastic anecdotes, facts contrary to all probability; but after attacking the evidence on which such absurdities relied, it now learned that all extraordinary facts must always be rejected, however impressive the evidence in their favour, unless this can truly turn the scale against the weight of their physical or moral probability.

Thus all the intellectual activities of man, however different they may be in their aims, their methods, or the qualities of mind they exact, have combined to further the progress of human reason. Indeed, the whole system of human labour is like a well-made machine, whose several parts have been systematically distinguished but none the less, being intimately bound together, form a single whole, and work towards a single end.

Turning now our attention to the human race in general, we shall show how the discovery of the correct method of procedure in the sciences, the growth of scientific theories, their application to every part of the natural world, to the subject of every human need, the lines of communication established between one science and another, the great number of men who cultivate the sciences, and most important of all, the spread of printing, how together all these advances ensure that no science will ever fall below the point it has reached. We shall point out that the principles of philosophy, the slogans of liberty, the recognition of the true rights of man and his real interests, have spread through far too great a number of nations, and now direct in each of them the opinions of far too great a number of enlightened men, for us to fear that they will ever be allowed to relapse into oblivion. And indeed what reason could we have for fear, when we consider that the languages most widely spoken are the languages of the two peoples who enjoy liberty to the fullest extent and who best understand its principles, and that no league of tyrants, no political intrigues, could prevent the resolute defence, in these two languages, of the rights of reason and of liberty?

But although everything tells us that the human race will never relapse into its former state of barbarism, although everything combines to reassure us against that corrupt and cowardly political theory which would condemn it to oscillate forever between truth and error, liberty and servitude, nevertheless we still see the forces of enlightenment in possession of no more than a very small portion of the globe, and the truly enlightened vastly outnumbered by the great mass of men who are still given over to ignorance and prejudice. We still see vast areas in which men groan in slavery, vast areas offering the spectacle of nations either degraded by the vices of a civilization whose progress is impeded by corruption, or still vegetating in the infant condition of early times. We observe that the labours of recent ages have done much for the progress of the human mind, but little for the perfection of the human race; that they have done much for the honour of man, something for his liberty, but so far almost nothing for his happiness. At a few points our eyes are dazzled with a brilliant light; but thick darkness still covers an immense stretch of the horizon. There are a few circumstances from which the philosopher can take consolation; but he is still afflicted by the spectacle of the stupidity, slavery, barbarism and extravagance of mankind; and the friend of humanity can find unmixed pleasure only in tasting the sweet delights of hope for the future.

Such are the subjects that ought to enter into a historical sketch of the progress of the human mind. In presenting it,

we shall endeavour above all to exhibit the influence of this
progress on the opinions and the welfare of the great mass
of the people, in the different nations, at the different stages
of their political existence. We shall endeavour to exhibit the
truths they have learnt, the errors from which they have
been freed, the habits of virtue they have contracted, and
the developments in their capacities that have established a
more fortunate relation between their wants and these
capacities; and, then by way of contrast, the prejudices that
have enslaved them, the political or religious superstitions
with which they have been infected, the vices with which
they have been corrupted by ignorance or tyranny, and the
misery to which they have been subjected either by force or
by their own degradation.

Up till now, the history of politics, like that of philosophy
or of science, has been the history of only a few individuals:
that which really constitutes the human race, the vast mass
of families living for the most part on the fruits of their
labour, has been forgotten, and even of those who follow
public professions, and work not for themselves but for
society, who are engaged in teaching, ruling, protecting
or healing others, it is only the leaders who have held the
eye of the historian.

In writing the history of individuals, it is enough to
collect facts; but the history of a group of men must be
supported by observations; and to select these observations
and to fasten upon their essential features enlightenment is
necessary, and, to use them to good effect, philosophy in the
same measure.

Moreover, these observations relate to quite ordinary
matters, which lie open to every eye, and which anyone
who so desires can find out about by himself. Consequently
almost all the observations that have been collected have
been made by travellers or foreigners; for facts that are
regarded as common-place in their own country, become
for them objects of curiosity. But unfortunately travellers

are nearly always inaccurate observers; they observe things too hastily, through the prejudices of their own country or of that in which they are travelling; they discuss them with those into whose company chance has thrown them, and what they are told is nearly always dictated by self interest, by the spirit of party, by patriotic pride, or merely by the mood of the moment.

Thus it is not only to the servility of historians, as has been said with justice about the official historians of monarchs, that we must attribute the scarcity of records that would allow us to follow this, the most important chapter in the history of man.

These records we can supplement, but only imperfectly, by a study of legal systems, of the practical principles of polices and public economy, and of religion and superstition in general. For there can be such a vast discrepancy between the law in writing and the law applied, between the principles of rulers and their practice as modified by the will of their subjects, between a social institution in the minds of those who conceive it and the same institution when its provisions are realized in practice, between the religion of books and the religion of the people, between the apparently universal acceptance of a superstition and the support which it can in fact command, that the actual effects may bear no relation whatever to their apparent and generally accepted causes as studied by the historian.

It is this most obscure and neglected chapter of the history of the human race, for which we can gather so little material from records, that must occupy the fore-ground of our picture; and whether we are concerned with a discovery, an important theory, a new legal system, or a political revolution, we shall endeavour to determine its consequences for the majority in each society. For it is there that one finds the true subject matter of philosophy, for all intermediate consequences may be ignored except in so far as they eventually influence the greater mass of the human race.

It is only when we come to this final link in the chain that our contemplation of historical events and the reflections that occur to us are of true utility. Only then can we appreciate men's true claims to fame, and can take real pleasure in the progress of their reason; only then can we truly judge the perfection of the human race.

The idea that everything must be considered in relation to this single point of reference is dictated both by justice and by reason. Nevertheless one might be tempted to regard it as fantastic. But one would be wrong. To show this is so, we have only to cite two striking examples.

The man who tills our soil owes his enjoyment of the commonest goods, which plentifully supply his needs, to the long-continued labours of industry assisted by science: and his enjoyment of these goods can be traced even further back, to the victory of Salamis, but for which the shadows of Oriental despotism threatened to engulf the earth. Similarly, the mariner who is preserved from shipwreck by precise observations of longitude, owes his life to a theory which can be traced back, through a chain of truths, to discoveries made in the school of Plato, and thereafter buried for twenty centuries in total disuse.

THE TENTH STAGE

The future progress of the human mind

IF MAN CAN, with almost complete assurance, predict phenomena when he knows their laws, and if, even when he does
not, he can still, with great expectation of success, forecast
the future on the basis of his experience of the past, why,
then, should it be regarded as a fantastic undertaking to
sketch, with some pretence to truth, the future destiny of
man on the basis of his history? The sole foundation for
belief in the natural sciences is this idea, that the general
laws directing the phenomena of the universe, known or
unknown, are necessary and constant. Why should this
principle be any less true for the development of the intellectual and moral faculties of man than for the other operations of nature? Since beliefs founded on past experience
of like conditions provide the only rule of conduct for the
wisest of men, why should the philosopher be forbidden to
base his conjectures on these same foundations, so long as
he does not attribute to them a certainty superior to that
warranted by the number, the constancy, and the accuracy
of his observations?

Our hopes for the future condition of the human race can
be subsumed under three important heads: the abolition of
inequality between nations, the progress of equality within
each nation, and the true perfection of mankind. Will all
nations one day attain that state of civilization which the
most enlightened, the freest and the least burdened by
prejudices, such as the French and the Anglo-Americans,
have attained already? Will the vast gulf that separates

these peoples from the slavery of nations under the rule of monarchs, from the barbarism of African tribes, from the ignorance of savages, little by little disappear?

Is there on the face of the earth a nation whose inhabitants have been debarred by nature herself from the enjoyment of freedom and the exercise of reason?

Are those differences which have hitherto been seen in every civilized country in respect of the enlightenment, the resources, and the wealth enjoyed by the different classes into which it is divided, is that inequality between men which was aggravated or perhaps produced by the earliest progress of society, are these part of civilization itself, or are they due to the present imperfections of the social art? Will they necessarily decrease and ultimately make way for a real equality, the final end of the social art, in which even the effects of the natural differences between men will be mitigated and the only kind of inequality to persist will be that which is in the interests of all and which favours the progress of civilization, of education, and of industry, without entailing either poverty, humiliation, or dependence? In other words, will men approach a condition in which everyone will have the knowledge necessary to conduct himself in the ordinary affairs of life, according to the light of his own reason, to preserve his mind free from prejudice, to understand his rights and to exercise them in accordance with his conscience and his creed; in which everyone will become able, through the development of his faculties, to find the means of providing for his needs; and in which at last misery and folly will be the exception, and no longer the habitual lot of a section of society?

Is the human race to better itself, either by discoveries in the sciences and the arts, and so in the means to individual welfare and general prosperity; or by progress in the principles of conduct or practical morality; or by a true perfection of the intellectual, moral, or physical faculties of man, an improvement which may result from a perfection either of the instruments used to heighten the intensity of these faculties and to direct their use or of the natural constitution of man?

In answering these three questions we shall find in the experience of the past, in the observation of the progress that the sciences and civilization have already made, in the analysis of the progress of the human mind and of the development of its faculties, the strongest reasons for believing that nature has set no limit to the realization of our hopes.

If we glance at the state of the world today we see first of all that in Europe the principles of the French constitution are already those of all enlightened men. We see them too widely propagated, too seriously professed, for priests and despots to prevent their gradual penetration even into the hovels of their slaves; there they will soon awaken in these slaves the remnants of their common sense and inspire them with that smouldering indignation which not even constant humiliation and fear can smother in the soul of the oppressed.

As we move from nation to nation, we can see in each what special obstacles impede this revolution and what attitudes of mind favour it. We can distinguish the nations where we may expect it to be introduced gently by the perhaps belated wisdom of their governments, and those nations where its violence intensified by their resistance must involve all alike in a swift and terrible convulsion.

Can we doubt that either common sense or the senseless discords of European nations will add to the effects of the slow but inexorable progress of their colonies, and will soon bring about the independence of the New World? And then will not the European population in these colonies, spreading rapidly over that enormous land, either civilize or peacefully remove the savage nations who still inhabit vast tracts of its land?

Survey the history of our settlements and commercial

undertakings in Africa or in Asia, and you will see how our trade monopolies, our treachery, our murderous contempt for men of another colour or creed, the insolence of our usurpations, the intrigues or the exaggerated proselytic zeal of our priests, have destroyed the respect and goodwill that the superiority of our knowledge and the benefits of our commerce at first won for us in the eyes of the inhabitants. But doubtless the moment approaches when, no longer presenting ourselves as always either tyrants or corrupters, we shall become for them the beneficent instruments of their freedom.

The sugar industry, establishing itself throughout the immense continent of Africa, will destroy the shameful exploitation which has corrupted and depopulated that continent for the last two centuries.

Already in Great Britain, friends of humanity have set us an example; and if the Machiavellian government of that country has been restrained by public opinion from offering any opposition, what may we not expect of this same spirit, once the reform of a servile and venal constitution has led to a government worthy of a humane and generous nation? Will not France hasten to imitate such undertakings dictated by philanthropy and the true self-interest of Europe alike? Trading stations have been set up in the French islands, in Guiana and in some English possessions, and soon we shall see the downfall of the monopoly that the Dutch have sustained with so much treachery, persecution and crime. The nations of Europe will finally learn that monopolistic companies are nothing more than a tax imposed upon them in order to provide their governments with a new instrument of tyranny.

So the peoples of Europe, confining themselves to free trade, understanding their own rights too well to show contempt for those of other peoples, will respect this independence, which until now they have so insolently violated. Their settlements, no longer filled with government hirelings hastening, under the cloak of place or privilege, to amass treasure by brigandry and deceit, so as to be able to return to Europe and purchase titles and honour, will now be peopled with men of industrious habit, seeking in these propitious climates the wealth that eluded them at home. The love of freedom will retain them there, ambition will no longer recall them, and what have been no better than the counting-houses of brigands will become colonies of citizens propagating throughout Africa and Asia the principles and the practice of liberty, knowledge and reason, that they have brought from Europe. We shall see the monks who brought only shameful superstition to these peoples and aroused their antagonism by the threat of yet another tyranny, replaced by men occupied in propagating amongst them the truths that will promote their happiness and in teaching them about their interests and their rights. Zeal for the truth is also one of the passions, and it will turn its efforts to distant lands, once there are no longer at home any crass prejudices to combat, any shameful errors to dissipate.

These vast lands are inhabited partly by large tribes who need only assistance from us to become civilized, who wait only to find brothers amongst the European nations to become their friends and pupils; partly by races oppressed by sacred despots or dull-witted conquerors, and who for so many centuries have cried out to be liberated; partly by tribes living in a condition of almost total savagery in a climate whose harshness repels the sweet blessings of civilization and deters those who would teach them its benefits; and finally, by conquering hordes who know no other law but force, no other profession but piracy. The progress of these two last classes of people will be slower and stormier; and perhaps it will even be that, reduced in number as they are driven back by civilized nations, they will finally disappear imperceptibly before them or merge into them.

N

We shall point out how these events will be the inevitable result not merely of the progress of Europe but also of the freedom that the French and the North American Republics can, and in their own real interest should, grant to the trade of Africa and Asia; and how they must of necessity be born either of a new-found wisdom on the part of the European nations, or of their obstinate attachment to mercantilist prejudices.

We shall show that there is only one event, a new invasion of Asia by the Tartars, that could prevent this revolution, and that this event is now impossible. Meanwhile everything forecasts the imminent decadence of the great religions of the East, which in most countries have been made over to the people, and, not uncontaminated by the corruption of their ministers, are in some already regarded by the ruling classes as mere political inventions; in consequence of which they are now powerless to retain human reason in hopeless bondage, in eternal infancy.

The progress of these peoples is likely to be more rapid and certain than our own because they can receive from us everything that we have had to find out for ourselves, and in order to understand those simple truths and infallible methods which we have acquired only after long error, all that they need to do is to follow the expositions and proofs that appear in our speeches and writings. If the progress of the Greeks was lost to later nations, this was because of the absence of any form of communication between the different peoples, and for this we must blame the tyrannical domination of the Romans. But when mutual needs have brought all men together, and the great powers have established equality between societies as well as between individuals and have raised respect for the independence of weak states and sympathy for ignorance and misery to the rank of political principles, when maxims that favour action and energy have ousted those which would compress the province of human faculties, will it then be possible to fear that there are still places in the world inaccessible to enlightenment, or that despotism in its pride can raise barriers against truth that are insurmountable for long?

The time will therefore come when the sun will shine only on free men who know no other master but their reason; when tyrants and slaves, priests and their stupid or hypocritical instruments will exist only in works of history and on the stage; and when we shall think of them only to pity their victims and their dupes; to maintain ourselves in a state of vigilance by thinking on their excesses; and to learn how to recognize and so to destroy, by force of reason, the first seeds of tyranny and superstition, should they ever dare to reappear amongst us.

In looking at the history of societies we shall have had occasion to observe that there is often a great difference between the rights that the law allows its citizens and the rights that they actually enjoy, and, again, between the equality established by political codes and that which in fact exists amongst individuals: and we shall have noticed that these differences were one of the principal causes of the destruction of freedom in the Ancient republics, of the storms that troubled them, and of the weakness that delivered them over to foreign tyrants.

These differences have three main causes: inequality in wealth; inequality in status between the man whose means of subsistence are hereditary and the man whose means are dependent on the length of his life, or, rather, on that part of his life in which he is capable of work; and, finally, inequality in education.

We therefore need to show that these three sorts of real inequality must constantly diminish without however disappearing altogether: for they are the result of natural and necessary causes which it would be foolish and dangerous to wish to eradicate; and one could not even attempt to bring about the entire disappearance of their effects without introducing even more fecund sources of inequality, without striking more direct and more fatal blows at the rights of man.

It is easy to prove that wealth has a natural tendency to equality, and that any excessive disproportion could not exist or at least would rapidly disappear if civil laws did not provide artificial ways of perpetuating and uniting fortunes; if free trade and industry were allowed to remove the advantages that accrued wealth derives from any restrictive law or fiscal privilege; if taxes on covenants, the restrictions placed on their free employment, their subjection to tiresome formalities and the uncertainty and inevitable expense involved in implementing them did not hamper the activity of the poor man and swallow up his meagre capital; if the administration of the country did not afford some men ways of making their fortune that were closed to other citizens; if prejudice and avarice, so common in old age, did not preside over the making of marriages; and if, in a society enjoying simpler manners and more sensible institutions, wealth ceased to be a means of satisfying vanity and ambition, and if the equally misguided notions of austerity, which condemn spending money in the cultivation of the more delicate pleasures, no longer insisted on the hoarding of all one's earnings.

Let us turn to the enlightened nations of Europe, and observe the size of their present populations in relation to the size of their territories. Let us consider, in agriculture and industry the proportion that holds between labour and the means of subsistence, and we shall see that it would be impossible for those means to be kept at their present level and consequently for the population to be kept at its present size if a great number of individuals were not almost entirely dependent for the maintenance of themselves and their family either on their own labour or on the interest from capital invested so as to make their labour more productive. Now both these sources of income depend on the life and even on the health of the head of the family. They

provide what is rather like a life annuity, save that it is more
dependent on chance; and in consequence there is a very
real difference between people living like this and those
whose resources are not at all subject to the same risks, who
live either on revenue from land, or on the interest on capital which is almost independent of their own labour.

Here then is a necessary cause of inequality, of dependence and even of misery, which ceaselessly threatens the
most numerous and most active class in our society.

We shall point out how it can be in great part eradicated
by guaranteeing people in old age a means of livelihood produced partly by their own savings and partly by the savings
of others who make the same outlay, but who die before they
need to reap the reward; or, again, on the same principle of
compensation, by securing for widows and orphans an income which is the same and costs the same for those families
which suffer an early loss and for those which suffer it later;
or again by providing all children with the capital necessary
for the full use of their labour, available at the age
when they start work and found a family, a capital which
increases at the expense of those whom premature death
prevents from reaching this age. It is to the application of
the calculus to the probabilities of life and the investment of
money that we owe the idea of these methods which have
already been successful, although they have not been applied
in a sufficiently comprehensive and exhaustive fashion to
render them really useful, not merely to a few individuals,
but to society as a whole, by making it possible to prevent
those periodic disasters which strike at so many families and
which are such a recurrent source of misery and suffering.

We shall point out that schemes of this nature, which can
be organized in the name of the social authority and become
one of its greatest benefits, can also be the work of private
associations, which will be formed without any real risk,
once the principles for the proper working of these schemes
have been widely diffused and the mistakes which have

been the undoing of a large number of these associations no longer hold terrors for us.

[We shall reveal other methods of ensuring this equality, either by seeing that credit is no longer the exclusive privilege of great wealth, but that it has another and no less sound foundation; or by making industrial progress and commercial activity more independent of the existence of the great capitalists. And once again, it is to the application of the calculus that we shall be indebted for such methods.]

The degree of equality in education that we can reasonably hope to attain, but that should be adequate, is that which excludes all dependence, either forced or voluntary. We shall show how this condition can be easily attained in the present state of human knowledge even by those who can study only for a small number of years in childhood, and then during the rest of their life in their few hours of leisure. We shall prove that, by a suitable choice of syllabus and of methods of education, we can teach the citizen everything that he needs to know in order to be able to manage his household, administer his affairs and employ his labour and his faculties in freedom; to know his rights and to be able to exercise them · to be acquainted with his duties and fulfil them satisfactorily; to judge his own and other men's actions according to his own lights and to be a stranger to none of the high and delicate feelings which honour human nature; not to be in a state of blind dependence upon those to whom he must entrust his affairs or the exercise of his rights; to be in a proper condition to choose and supervise them; to be no longer the dupe of those popular errors which torment man with superstitious fears and chimerical hopes; to defend himself against prejudice by the strength of his reason alone; and, finally, to escape the deceits of charlatans who would lay snares for his fortune, his health, his freedom of thought and his conscience under the pretext of granting him health, wealth and salvation.

From such time onwards the inhabitants of a single country will no longer be distinguished by their use of a crude or refined language; they will be able to govern themselves according to their own knowledge; they will no longer be limited to a mechanical knowledge of the procedures of the arts or of professional routine; they will no longer depend for every trivial piece of business, every insignificant matter of instruction on clever men who rule over them in virtue of their necessary superiority; and so they will attain a real equality, since differences in enlightenment or talent can no longer raise a barrier between men who understand each other's feelings, ideas and language, some of whom may wish to be taught by others but, to do so, will have no need to be controlled by them, or who may wish to confide the care of government to the ablest of their number but will not be compelled to yield them absolute power in a spirit of blind confidence.

This kind of supervision has advantages even for those who do not exercise it, since it is employed for them and not against them. Natural differences of ability between men whose understanding has not been cultivated give rise, even in savage tribes, to charlatans and dupes, to clever men and men readily deceived. These same differences are truly universal, but now they are differences only between men of learning and upright men who know the value of learning without being dazzled by it; or between talent or genius and the common sense which can appreciate and benefit from them ; so that even if these natural differences were greater, and more extensive than they are, they would be only the more influential in improving the relations between men and promoting what is advantageous for their independence and happiness.

These various causes of equality do not act in isolation; they unite, combine and support each other and so their cumulative effects are stronger, surer and more constant. With greater equality of education there will be greater equality in industry and so in wealth; equality in wealth necessarily leads to equality in education: and equality between the nations and equality within a single nation are mutually dependent.

So we might say that a well directed system of education rectifies natural inequality in ability instead of strengthening it, just as good laws remedy natural inequality in the means of subsistence, and just as in societies where laws have brought about this same equality, liberty, though subject to a regular constitution, will be more widespread, more complete than in the total independence of savage life. Then the social art will have fulfilled its aim, that of assuring and extending to all men enjoyment of the common rights to which they are called by nature.

The real advantages that should result from this progress, of which we can entertain a hope that is almost a certainty, can have no other term than that of the absolute perfection of the human race; since, as the various kinds of equality come to work in its favour by producing ampler sources of supply, more extensive education, more complete liberty, so equality will be more real and will embrace everything which is really of importance for the happiness of human beings.

It is therefore only by examining the progress and the laws of this perfection that we shall be able to understand the extent or the limits of our hopes.

No-one has ever believed that the mind can gain knowledge of all the facts of nature or attain the ultimate means of precision in the measurement, or in the analysis of the facts of nature, the relations between objects and all the possible combinations of ideas. Even the relations between magnitudes, the mere notion of quantity or extension, taken in its fullest comprehension, gives rise to a system so vast that it will never be mastered by the human mind in its entirety, that there will always be a part of it, always indeed the larger part of it that will remain for ever unknown.

People have believed that man can never know more than
a part of the objects that the nature of his intelligence allows
him to understand, and that he must in the end arrive at a
point where the number and complexity of the objects that
he already knows have absorbed all his strength so that any
further progress must be completely impossible.

But since, as the number of known facts increases, the
human mind learns how to classify them and to subsume
them under more general facts, and, at the same time, the
instruments and methods employed in their observation and
their exact measurement acquire a new precision; since, as
more relations between various objects become known,
man is able to reduce them to more general relations, to
express them more simply, and to present them in such a
way that it is possible to grasp a greater number of them
with the same degree of intellectual ability and the same
amount of application; since, as the mind learns to understand more complicated combinations of ideas, simpler
formulae soon reduce their complexity; so truths that were
discovered only by great effort, that could at first only be
understood by men capable of profound thought, are soon
developed and proved by methods that are not beyond the
reach of common intelligence. If the methods which have
led to these new combinations of ideas are ever exhausted,
if their application to hitherto unsolved questions should
demand exertions greater than either the time or the capacity of the learned would permit, some method of a greater
generality or simplicity will be found so that genius can
continue undisturbed on its path. The strength and the
limits of man's intelligence may remain unaltered; and yet
the instruments that he uses will increase and improve, the
language that fixes and determines his ideas will acquire
greater breadth and precision and, unlike mechanics where
an increase of force means a decrease of speed, the methods
that lead genius to the discovery of truth increase at once
the force and the speed of its operations.

Therefore, since these developments are themselves the necessary consequences of progress in detailed knowledge, and since the need for new methods in fact only arises in circumstances that give rise to new methods, it is evident that, within the body of the sciences of observation, calculation and experiment, the actual number of truths may always increase, and that every part of this body may develop, and yet man's faculties be of the same strength, activity and extent.

If we apply these general reflections to the various sciences, we can find in each of them examples of progressive improvement that will remove any doubts about what we may expect for the future. We shall point out in particular the progress that is both likely and imminent in those sciences which prejudice regards as all but exhausted. We shall give examples of the manner and extent of the precision and unity which could accrue to the whole system of human knowledge as the result of a more general and philosophical application of the sciences of calculation to the various branches of knowledge. We shall show how favourable to our hopes would be a more universal system of education by giving a greater number of people the elementary knowledge which could awaken their interest in a particular branch of study, and by providing conditions favourable to their progress in it; and how these hopes would be further raised, if more men possessed the means to devote themselves to these studies, for at present even in the most enlightened countries scarcely one in fifty of the people who have natural talents, receives the necessary education to develop them; and how, if this were done there would be a proportionate increase in the number of men destined by their discoveries to extend the boundaries of science.

We shall show how this equality in education and the equality which will come about between the different nations would accelerate the advance of these sciences whose progress depends on repeated observations over a large area;

what benefits would thereby accrue to mineralogy, botany, zoology and meteorology; and what a vast disproportion holds in all these sciences between the poverty of existing methods which have nevertheless led to useful and important new truths, and the wealth of those methods which man would then be able to employ.

We shall show how even the sciences in which discovery is the fruit of solitary meditation would benefit from being studied by a greater number of people, in the matter of those improvements in detail which do not demand the intellectual energy of an inventor but suggest themselves to mere reflection.

If we turn now to the arts, whose theory depends on these same sciences, we shall find that their progress depending as it does on that of theory, can have no other limits; that the procedures of the different arts can be perfected and simplified in the same way as the methods of the sciences; new instruments, machines and looms can add to man's strength and can improve at once the quality and the accuracy of his productions, and can diminish the time and labour that has to be expended on them. The obstacles still in the way of this progress will disappear, accidents will be foreseen and prevented, the insanitary conditions that are due either to the work itself or to the climate will be eliminated.

A very small amount of ground will be able to produce a great quantity of supplies of greater utility or higher quality; more goods will be obtained for a smaller outlay; the manufacture of articles will be achieved with less wastage in raw materials and will make better use of them. Every type of soil will produce those things which satisfy the greatest number of needs; of several alternative ways of satisfying needs of the same order, that will be chosen which satisfies the greatest number of people and which requires least labour and least expenditure. So, without the need for sacrifice, methods of preservation and economy in expenditure will improve in the wake of progress in the arts of producing and preparing supplies and making articles from them.

So not only will the same amount of ground support more people, but everyone will have less work to do, will produce more, and satisfy his wants more fully.

With all this progress in industry and welfare which establishes a happier proportion between men's talents and their needs, each successive generation will have larger possessions, either as a result of this progress or through the preservation of the products of industry; and so, as a consequence of the physical constitution of the human race, the number of people will increase. Might there not then come a moment when these necessary laws begin to work in a contrary direction; when, the number of people in the world finally exceeding the means of subsistence, there will in consequence ensue a continual diminution of happiness and population, a true retrogression, or at best an oscillation between good and bad? In societies that have reached this stage will not this oscillation be a perennial source of more or less periodic disaster? Will it not show that a point has been attained beyond which all further improvement is impossible, that the perfectibility of the human race has after long years arrived at a term beyond which it may never go?

There is doubtless no-one who does not think that such a time is still very far from us; but will it ever arrive? It is impossible to pronounce about the likelihood of an event that will occur only when the human species will have necessarily acquired a degree of knowledge of which we can have no inkling. And who would take it upon himself to predict the condition to which the art of converting the elements to the use of man may in time be brought?

But even if we agree that the limit will one day arrive, nothing follows from it that is in the least alarming as far as either the happiness of the human race or its indefinite perfectibility is concerned; if we consider that, before all this comes to pass, the progress of reason will have kept pace with that of the sciences, and that the absurd prejudices of superstition will have ceased to corrupt and degrade the moral code by its harsh doctrines instead of purifying and elevating it, we can assume that by then men will know that, if they have a duty towards those who are not yet born, that duty is not to give them existence but to give them happiness; their aim should be to promote the general welfare of the human race or of the society in which they live or of the family to which they belong, rather than foolishly to encumber the world with useless and wretched beings. It is, then, possible that there should be a limit to the amount of food that can be produced, and, consequently, to the size of the population of the world, without this involving that untimely destruction of some of those creatures who have been given life, which is so contrary to nature and to social prosperity.

Since the discovery, or rather the exact analysis of the first principles of metaphysics, morals and politics is still recent and was preceded by the knowledge of a large number of detailed truths, the false notion that they have thereby attained their destination, has gained ready acceptance; men imagine that, because there are no more crude errors to refute, no more fundamental truths to establish, nothing remains to be done.

But it is easy to see how imperfect is the present analysis of man's moral and intellectual faculties; how much further the knowledge of his duties which presumes a knowledge of the influence of his actions upon the welfare of his fellow men and upon the society to which he belongs, can still be increased through a more profound, more accurate, more considered observation of that influence; how many questions have to be solved, how many social relations to be examined, before we can have precise knowledge of the individual rights of man and the rights that the state confers upon each in regard to all. Have we yet ascertained at all accurately the limits of the rights that exist between different societies in times of war, or that are enjoyed by society over its members in times of trouble and schism, or that belong to individuals, or spontaneous associations at the moment of their original, free formation or of their necessary disintegration?

If we pass on to the theory which ought to direct the application of particular principles and serve as the foundation for the social art, do we not see the necessity of acquiring a precision that these elementary truths cannot possess so long as they are absolutely general? Have we yet reached the point when we can reckon as the only foundation of law either justice or a proved and acknowledged utility instead of the vague, uncertain, arbitrary views of alleged political expediency? Are we yet in possession of any precise rules for selecting out of the almost infinite variety of possible systems in which the general principles of equality and natural rights are respected, those which will best secure the preservation of these rights, which will afford the freest scope for their exercise and their enjoyment, and which will moreover insure the leisure and welfare of individuals and the strength, prosperity and peace of nations?

The application of the calculus of combinations and probabilities to these sciences promises even greater improvement, since it is the only way of achieving results of an almost mathematical exactitude and of assessing the degree of their probability or likelihood. Sometimes, it is true, the evidence upon which these results are based may lead us, without any calculation, at the first glance, to some general truth and teach us whether the effect produced by such-and-such a cause was or was not favourable, but if this evidence cannot be weighed and measured, and if these effects cannot be subjected to precise measurement, then we cannot know exactly how much good or evil they contain; or, again, if the good and evil nearly balance each other, if the difference between them is slight, we cannot pronounce with any

certainty to which side the balance really inclines. Without
the application of the calculus it would be almost impossible
to choose with any certainty between two combinations that
have the same purpose and between which there is no apparent difference in merit. Without the calculus these
sciences would always remain crude and limited for want of
instruments delicate enough to catch the fleeting truth, of
machines precise enough to plumb the depths where so
much that is of value to science lies hidden.

However, such an application, notwithstanding the happy
efforts of certain geometers, is still in its earliest stages: and
it will be left to the generations to come to use this source
of knowledge which is as inexhaustible as the calculus
itself, or as the number of combinations, relations and facts
that may be included in its sphere of operation.

There is another kind of progress within the sciences that
is no less important; and that is the perfection of scientific
language which is at present so vague and obscure. This improvement could be responsible for making the sciences
genuinely popular, even in their first rudiments. Genius
can triumph over the inexactitude of language as over other
obstacles and can recognize the truth through the strange
mask that hides or disguises it. But how can someone with
only a limited amount of leisure to devote to his education
master and retain even the simplest truths if they are dis-
torted by an imprecise language? The fewer the ideas that
he is able to acquire and combine, the more necessary is it
that they should be precise and exact. He has no fund of
knowledge stored up in his mind which he can draw upon
to protect himself from error, and his understanding, not
being strengthened and refined by long practice, cannot
catch such feeble rays of light as manage to penetrate the
obscurities, the ambiguities of an imperfect and perverted
language.

Until men progress in the practice as well as in the science
of morality, it will be impossible for them to attain any

insight into either the nature and development of the moral
sentiments, the principles of morality, the natural motives
that prompt their actions, or their own true interests either
as individuals or as members of society. Is not a mistaken
sense of interest the most common cause of actions contrary
to the general welfare? Is not the violence of our passions
often the result either of habits that we have adopted
through miscalculation, or of our ignorance how to restrain
them, tame them, deflect them, rule them?

Is not the habit of reflection upon conduct, of listening
to the deliverances of reason and conscience upon it, of exercising those gentle feelings which identify our happiness
with that of others, the necessary consequence of a well-
planned study of morality and of a greater equality in the
conditions of the social pact? Will not the free man's sense
of his own dignity and a system of education built upon a
deeper knowledge of our moral constitution, render common
to almost every man those principles of strict and unsullied
justice, those habits of an active and enlightened benevolence, of a fine and generous sensibility which nature has
implanted in the hearts of all and whose flowering waits only
upon the favourable influences of enlightenment and freedom? Just as the mathematical and physical sciences tend to
improve the arts that we use to satisfy our simplest needs, is
it not also part of the necessary order of nature that the moral
and political sciences should exercise a similar influence
upon the motives that direct our feelings and our actions?

What are we to expect from the perfection of laws and
public institutions, consequent upon the progress of those
sciences, but the reconciliation, the identification of the
interests of each with the interests of all? Has the social art
any other aim save that of destroying their apparent opposition? Will not a country's constitution and laws accord best
with the rights of reason and nature when the path of virtue
is no longer arduous and when the temptations that lead
men from it are few and feeble?

Is there any vicious habit, any practice contrary to good faith, any crime, whose origin and first cause cannot be traced back to the legislation, the institutions, the prejudices of the country wherein this habit, this practice, this crime can be observed? In short will not the general welfare that results from the progress of the useful arts once they are grounded on solid theory, or from the progress of legislation once it is rooted in the truths of political science, incline mankind to humanity, benevolence and justice? In other words, do not all these observations which I propose to develop further in my book, show that the moral goodness of man, the necessary consequence of his constitution, is capable of indefinite perfection like all his other faculties, and that nature has linked together in an unbreakable chain truth, happiness and virtue?

Among the causes of the progress of the human mind that are of the utmost importance to the general happiness, we must number the complete annihilation of the prejudices that have brought about an inequality of rights between the sexes, an inequality fatal even to the party in whose favour it works. It is vain for us to look for a justification of this principle in any differences of physical organization, intellect or moral sensibility between men and women. This inequality has its origin solely in an abuse of strength, and all the later sophistical attempts that have been made to excuse it are vain.

We shall show how the abolition of customs authorized, laws dictated by this prejudice, would add to the happiness of family life, would encourage the practice of the domestic virtues on which all other virtues are based, how it would favour the progress of education, and how, above all, it would bring about its wider diffusion; for not only would education be extended to women as well as to men, but it can only really be taken proper advantage of when it has the support and encouragement of the mothers of the family. Would not this belated tribute to equity and good sense,

o

put an end to a principle only too fecund of injustice, cruelty and crime, by removing the dangerous conflict between the strongest and most irrepressible of all natural inclinations and man's duty or the interests of society? Would it not produce what has until now been no more than a dream, national manners of a mildness and purity, formed not by proud asceticism, not by hypocrisy, not by the fear of shame or religious terrors but by freely contracted habits that are inspired by nature and acknowledged by reason?

Once people are enlightened they will know that they have the right to dispose of their own life and wealth as they choose; they will gradually learn to regard war as the most dreadful of scourges, the most terrible of crimes. The first wars to disappear will be those into which usurpers have forced their subjects in defence of their pretended hereditary rights.

Nations will learn that they cannot conquer other nations without losing their own liberty; that permanent confederations are their only means of preserving their independence; and that they should seek not power but security. Gradually mercantile prejudices will fade away: and a false sense of commercial interest will lose the fearful power it once had of drenching the earth in blood and of ruining nations under pretext of enriching them. When at last the nations come to agree on the principles of politics and morality, when in their own better interests they invite foreigners to share equally in all the benefits men enjoy either through the bounty of nature or by their own industry, then all the causes that produce and perpetuate national animosities and poison national relations will disappear one by one; and nothing will remain to encourage or even to arouse the fury of war.

Organizations more intelligently conceived than those projects of eternal peace which have filled the leisure and consoled the hearts of certain philosophers, will hasten the progress of the brotherhood of nations, and wars between countries will rank with assassinations as freakish atrocities, humiliating and vile in the eyes of nature and staining with indelible opprobrium the country or the age whose annals record them.

When we spoke of the fine arts in Greece, Italy and France, we observed that it was necessary to distinguish in artistic productions between what belonged properly to the progress of the art itself and what was due only to the talent of the individual artist. We shall here indicate what progress may still be expected in the arts as a result of the progress in philosophy and the sciences, of the increasing number of observations made about the aim, effects and methods of the arts, of the destruction of those prejudices which have formerly narrowed their sphere and even now hold them within the shackles of authority, shackles that science and philosophy have broken. We shall ask, whether, as some have thought, these means are exhausted, and the arts condemned to an eternal, monotonous imitation of their first models since the most sublime and moving beauty has already been apprehended, the happiest subjects treated, the simplest and most arresting ideas used, the most marked or most generous characters delineated, the liveliest intrinsic passions and their truest or most natural manifestations, the most striking truths and the most brilliant images already exploited.

We shall see that this opinion is a mere prejudice, born of the habit, which is prevalent among artists and men of letters, of judging men, instead of enjoying their works. If the more reflective pleasure of comparing the products of different ages and countries and admiring the success and energy of the efforts of genius will probably be lost, the pleasure to be derived from the actual contemplation of works of art as such will be just as vivid as ever, even though the author may no longer deserve the same credit for having achieved such perfection. As works of art genuinely worthy of preservation increase in number, and become more perfect, each successive generation will devote its attention and admiration to those which really deserve preference, and the rest will unobtrusively fall into oblivion; the pleasure to be derived from the simpler, more striking, more accessible aspects of beauty will exist no less for posterity although they will be found only in the latest works.

The progress of the sciences ensures the progress of the art of education which in turn advances that of the sciences. This reciprocal influence, whose activity is ceaselessly renewed, deserves to be seen as one of the most powerful and active causes working for the perfection of mankind. At the present time a young man on leaving school may know more of the principles of mathematics than Newton ever learnt in years of study or discovered by dint of genius, and he may use the calculus with a facility then unknown. The same observation, with certain reservations, applies to all the sciences. As each advances, the methods of expressing a large number of proofs in a more economical fashion and so of making their comprehension an easier matter, advance with it. So, in spite of the progress of science, not only do men of the same ability find themselves at the same age on a level with the existing state of science, but with every generation, that which can be acquired in a certain time with a certain degree of intelligence and a certain amount of concentration will be permanently on the increase, and, as the elementary part of each science to which all men may attain grows and grows, it will more and more include all the knowledge necessary for each man to know for the conduct of the ordinary events of his life, and will support him in the free and independent exercise of his reason.

In the political sciences there are some truths that, with free people (that is to say, with certain generations in all countries) can be of use only if they are widely known and acknowledged. So the influence of these sciences upon the freedom and prosperity of nations must in some degree be measured by the number of truths that, as a result of elementary instruction, are common knowledge; the swelling progress of elementary instruction, connected with the necessary progress of these sciences promises us an improvement in the destiny of the human race, which may be regarded as indefinite, since it can have no other limits than that of this same progress.

We have still to consider two other general methods which will influence both the perfection of education and that of the sciences. One is the more extensive and less imperfect use of what we might call technical methods; the other is the setting up of a universal language.

I mean by technical methods the art of arranging a large number of subjects in a system so that we may straightway grasp their relations, quickly perceive their combinations, and readily form new combinations out of them.

We shall develop the principles and examine the utility of this art, which is still in its infancy, and which, as it improves, will enable us, within the compass of a small chart, to set out what could possibly not be expressed so well in a whole book, or, what is still more valuable, to present isolated facts in such a way as to allow us to deduce their general consequences. We shall see how by means of a small number of these charts, whose use can easily be learned, men who have not been sufficiently educated to be able to absorb details useful to them in ordinary life, may now be able to master them when the need arises; and how these methods may likewise be of benefit to elementary education itself in all those branches where it is concerned either with a regular system of truths or with a series of observations and facts.

A universal language is that which expresses by signs either real objects themselves, or well-defined collections composed of simple and general ideas, which are found to be the same or may arise in a similar form in the minds of all men, or the general relations holding between these ideas, the operations of the human mind, or the operations peculiar to the individual sciences, or the procedures of the arts. So people who become acquainted with these signs, the ways to combine them and the rules for forming them will understand what is written in this language and will be able to read it as easily as their own language.

It is obvious that this language might be used to set out the theory of a science or the rules of an art, to describe a new observation or experiment, the invention of a procedure, the discovery of a truth or a method; and that, as in algebra, when one has to make use of a new sign, those already known provide the means of explaining its import.

Such a language has not the disadvantages of a scientific idiom different from the vernacular. We have already observed that the use of such an idiom would necessarily divide society into two unequal classes, the one composed of men who, understanding this language, would possess the key to all the sciences, the other of men who, unable to acquire it, would therefore find themselves almost completely unable to acquire enlightenment. In contrast to this, a universal language would be learnt, like that of algebra, along with the science itself; the sign would be learnt at the same time as the object, idea or operation that it designates. He who, having mastered the elements of a science, would like to know more of it, would find in books not only truths he could understand by means of the signs whose import he has learnt, but also the explanation of such further signs as he needs in order to go on to other truths.

We shall show that the formation of such a language, if confined to the expression of those simple, precise propositions which form the system of a science or the practice of an art, is no chimerical scheme; that even at the present time it could be readily introduced to deal with a large number of objects; and that, indeed, the chief obstacle that would prevent its extension to others would be the humiliation of having to admit how very few precise ideas and accurate, unambiguous notions we actually possess.

We shall show that this language, ever improving and broadening its scope all the while, would be the means of giving to every subject embraced by the human intelligence, a precision and a rigour that would make knowledge of the truth easy and error almost impossible. Then the progress of every science would be as sure as that of mathematics, and the propositions that compose it would acquire a geometrical certainty, as far, that is, as is possible granted the nature of its aim and method.

All the causes that contribute to the perfection of the human race, all the means that ensure it must by their very nature exercise a perpetual influence and always increase their sphere of action. The proofs of this we have given and in the great work they will derive additional force from elaboration. We may conclude then that the perfectibility of man is indefinite. Meanwhile we have considered him as possessing the natural faculties and organization that he has at present. How much greater would be the certainty, how must vaster the scheme of our hopes if we could believe that these natural faculties themselves and this organization could also be improved? This is the last question that remains for us to ask ourselves.

Organic perfectibility or deterioration amongst the various strains in the vegetable and animal kingdom can be regarded as one of the general laws of nature. This law also applies to the human race. No-one can doubt that, as preventitive medicine improves and food and housing become healthier, as a way of life is established that develops our physical powers by exercise without ruining them by excess, as the two most virulent causes of deterioration, misery and excessive wealth, are eliminated, the average length of human life will be increased and a better health and a stronger physical constitution will be ensured. The improvement of medical practice, which will become more efficacious with the progress of reason and of the social order, will mean the end of infectious and hereditary diseases and illnesses brought on by climate, food, or working conditions. It is reasonable to hope that all other diseases may likewise disappear as their distant causes are discovered. Would it be absurd then to suppose that this perfection of the human species might be capable of indefinite progress; that the day will come when death will be due only to extraordinary accidents or to the decay of the vital forces, and that ultimately the average span between birth and decay will have no assignable value? Certainly man will not become immortal, but will not the interval between the first breath that he draws and the time when in the natural course of events, without disease or accident, he expires, increase indefinitely? Since we are now speaking of a progress that can be represented with some accuracy in figures or on a graph, we shall take this opportunity of explaining the two meanings that can be attached to the word *indefinite*.

In truth, this average span of life which we suppose will increase indefinitely as time passes, may grow in conformity either with a law such that it continually approaches a limitless length but without ever reaching it, or with a law such that through the centuries it reaches a length greater than any determinate quantity that we may assign to it as its limit. In the latter case such an increase is truly indefinite in the strictest sense of the word, since there is no term on this side of which it must of necessity stop. In the former case it is equally indefinite in relation to us, if we cannot fix the limit it always approaches without ever reaching, and particularly if, knowing only that it will never stop, we are ignorant in which of the two senses the term 'indefinite' can be applied to it. Such is the present condition of our knowledge as far as the perfectibility of the human race is concerned; such is the sense in which we may call it indefinite.

So, in the example under consideration, we are bound to believe that the average length of human life will for ever increase unless this is prevented by physical revolutions; we do not know what the limit is which it can never exceed.

We cannot tell even whether the general laws of nature have determined such a limit or not.

But are not our physical faculties and the strength, dexterity and acuteness of our senses, to be numbered among the qualities whose perfection in the individual may be transmitted? Observation of the various breeds of domestic animals inclines us to believe that they are, and we can confirm this by direct observation of the human race.

Finally may we not extend such hopes to the intellectual and moral faculties? May not our parents, who transmit to us the benefits or disadvantages of their constitution, and from whom we receive our shape and features, as well as our tendencies to certain physical affections, hand on to us also that part of the physical organization which determines the intellect, the power of the brain, the ardour of the soul or the moral sensibility? Is it not probable that education, in perfecting these qualities, will at the same time influence, modify and perfect the organization itself? Analogy, investigation of the human faculties and the study of certain facts, all seem to give substance to such conjectures which would further push back the boundaries of our hopes.

These are the questions with which we shall conclude this final stage. How consoling for the philosopher who laments the errors, the crimes, the injustices which still pollute the earth and of which he is often the victim is this view of the human race, emancipated from its shackles, released from the empire of fate and from that of the enemies of its progress, advancing with a firm and sure step along the path of truth, virtue and happiness! It is the contemplation of this prospect that rewards him for all his efforts to assist the progress of reason and the defence of liberty. He dares to regard these strivings as part of the eternal chain of human destiny; and in this persuasion he is filled with the true delight of virtue and the pleasure of having done some lasting good which fate can never destroy by a sinister stroke of revenge, by calling back the reign of slavery and prejudice. Such contemplation is for him an asylum, in which the memory of his persecutors cannot pursue him; there he lives in thought with man restored to his natural rights and dignity, forgets man tormented and corrupted by greed, fear or envy; there he lives with his peers in an Elysium created by reason and graced by the purest pleasures known to the love of mankind.